PUT
RESULTS
FIRST

*Practical steps to harness
the power of destination*

HAL WILLIAMS

CREATOR, RESULTS 1ST

Book design by The Troy Book Makers

Printed in the United States of America
The Troy Book Makers • Troy, New York • thetroybookmakers.com

To order additional books, contact your favorite bookstore. For discounts and reader support services, go to **www.results1st.org.**

ISBN: 978-1-61468-874-7

For Pam, my love for a lifetime

TABLE OF CONTENTS

Preface..vii

Introduction.. 1

Part I: Five Acts for Success.................................. 9

Chapter 1: Define Success and Set Targets 11

Chapter 2: Track to Success..................................... 32

Chapter 3: Verify Achievement 49

Chapter 4: Learn and Change 80

Chapter 5: Communicate by Accomplishment 92

Part II: Acting Out 109

Chapter 6: Keep Your Program Live Longer................ 111

Chapter 7: Find the Sparkplugs................................ 120

Chapter 8: Try Something Else 127

Chapter 9: Decrease Your Cost Per Gain 137

Chapter 10: Move the Needle 145

Part III: Pivots in Formats 159

Chapter 11: The Organization Chart 161

Chapter 12: The Job Description 169

Chapter 13: The Budget 175

Chapter 14: The Resume 180

Chapter 15: The Strategic Plan 190

Chapter 16: The Logic Model 202

Chapter 17: The Proposal 210

Part IV: New Directions in Where the Money Goes 221

Chapter 18: Partnerships, Coalitions, Initiatives, Collaborations 223

Chapter 19: Diversity, Equity, and Inclusion 236

Part V: Making Change 245

Chapter 20: The Road to Results First 247

Afterword: Join Results 1st in a Compact? 253

Acknowledgments 255

PREFACE

So what? These two words changed my life – professionally and personally. I met Hal as a participant in a leadership program he was guiding. He asked me to introduce myself and state what my organization achieved for those we served. I proudly answered that we served 2,000 people the prior year, which was a 100% increase from the 1,000 people served two years prior. I felt pretty good about my answer. Until he looked me in the eye and said, "so what?"

After I recovered from the initial shock, he continued, "So what you served 2,000 people. Did all 2,000 of those people gain anything? Were all 2,000 successful?" My answer was no. This encounter, and those two words, started me on my results journey.

Hal asked me to write this not because I am the established authority commenting on his work. Rather, I was and remain his student. I started as a client when I was the CEO of Neuro Challenge Foundation for Parkinson's based out of Sarasota, FL. His approaches gave us breakthrough gains in defining, tracking, and verifying the gains our clients experienced from our programs.

I was both thrilled and deeply humbled when Hal asked me if I would like to start an organization to carry on his tools and concepts. We created together Results 1st. In 2023, three years after launching Results 1st, we are pleased that over 60 nonprofits and foundations report that we added great value to their achievement. I am especially proud of being seen as an option to present practices, formats, and approaches rather than another group that accepts them. Results need a different frame.

Hal speaks in the book of attributes such as energy, curiosity, and a solution focus. He is living proof that characteristics predict success more than knowledge or skills. His wisdom and his experience are greatly enhanced by who he is. The book reflects how personal and professional traits can come together if you are driven to build success in others more than in yourself.

Putting results first is transformative. It worked for me and now works for many others. Two aspects of our methodology are most meaningful to me. First, is the focus on action. Try something and build on what works. Results are a muscle. They are strengthened not by talking but by doing. Second, the result discipline applies to all sizes of groups, including those that are volunteer run with $50,000 annual budgets as well as those with a hundred or more staff.

My hope is that this book becomes your action guide for starting or strengthening your journey to success and the difference you and your organization make.

ROBYN FAUCY
CEO, Results 1st

INTRODUCTION

In 1992, I wrote a book with Arthur Webb and Bill Phillips called "Outcome Funding: A New Approach to Targeted Grantmaking." It was self-published by The Rensselaerville Institute and sold about 800 copies in its first year. A decade later, it sold 800 copies in one day. The book had not changed enough to explain this great rise in sales, but interest in results from social programs had expanded. Many more foundations, government agencies, and individual donors voiced a desire to know the difference their money had made.

Increased interest, however, has not led to widespread change in practice. Foundation proposal formats today often look little different than they did 40 years ago. Most nonprofits still only speak to their activities and ask participants if they are satisfied with them. On websites, data information on how many people achieved a specified gain from programs are three or more clicks away.

Most of the literature on nonprofit achievement speaks to concepts that float well above the realities of nonprofit leaders and staff. Books offer the four pillars, the three legs, the five keys. They do not tend to offer practical help, especially when it comes to achievement on the ground for a nonprofit and its participants.

1

They also tend to be for leaders, not the staff and volunteers who make all the difference. My first draft of this book drifted that way. It is so easy to draw visuals that show the tidy relationships among components and to let arrows stand for progress. Back on the ground, Hal!

I also found myself assuming the context of larger organizations. This misses the vast majority of nonprofits, which have small budgets and two or less paid staff. The Results 1st CEO, Robyn Faucy, calls us the action arm of everything nonprofits do. Motion begins with individuals who not only have energy but know how to harness it. Small size gets into gear easily as fast as does large size.

Here's the good news: virtually all work gets shorter and simpler when focused on results. Assessments are less complex, board and staff talking points are simpler. Reports are a few pages rather than 20. Results are not an addition to an already heaping nonprofit plate, but a way to chew on what is already there. They are the way you can do business. The premise is the title of the book: put results first. Once you have a clear aiming point, you can design programs to achieve your goal.

My further discovery is that the same results principles that help organizations can help individuals. Personal growth, for example, needs the same distinction between activities and results from activities. Tracking needs the same approach from another person to verify. The personal breakthroughs from results also benefit when they start with clarity on success. Many books speak eloquently on the traits that forecast personal success: energy, enthusiasm, stamina, compassion, grit. My quest is to put these in a results framework which applies who you are to what you achieve. That happens far more frequently with intention.

The book has five Parts.

PART I: I will present the five acts essential for becoming achievement-based as a person, group, or organization. Yes, my image is of acts, like a play, rather than chapters, like a manual. Drama brings the script and stage setting to life, and results come from real-time interactions with others.

Chapter 1: Define Success and Set Targets. When groups tell me they have trouble with outcomes, I find they largely have a problem in characterizing what they seek. The problem is not defining the problems they address, but defining the success they commit to achieve. I tackle the biggest problem I see: the failure to separate activities from accomplishments. Holding workshops or providing after-school enrichment hours are what you do, but the result is what people get from what you offer.

Chapter 2: Track to Success. How will you know, halfway through your program, that you are on course to hit your target by the set deadline? Sadly, I have heard groups and individuals answer this by saying they are halfway through their workplan and have spent half the money. This, of course, says nothing about how many participants are on course to achieve the intended gain. The pivot is a shift in focus from workplan, or what groups do, to milestones, which is what participants get from a program.

Chapter 3: Verify Achievement. How do you know what difference you made for your participants? While a few large projects need a full-scale evaluation, most can benefit from just asking the question: Did we hit our target? I consider a wide range of approaches that provide reasonable clarity on achievement. I take aim at the ubiquitous and anonymous surveys which provide the illusion of precision more than depth of experience. Impact lies deep. It takes result stories to turn anecdotes into data.

Chapter 4: Learn and Change. You have set targets then tracked and verified participant gains. How do you use that experience to increase results for the next cycle or year? Definition shifts from retaining information to using it. No one gets to say how much they have learned and how little they have changed. I introduce very simple tools for using experience to significantly increase gain. One is actually an attribute: curiosity. The best way to improve is to ask questions.

Chapter 5: Communicate by Accomplishment. Nothing is more suspect than the adage that results speak for themselves. They do not. You need people who can effectively articulate what you've achieved. Your vision, mission, beliefs, and program activities say what you do. Data points on success need equally clear formats, and I offer some.

PART II: I add five approaches that can greatly improve nonprofit accomplishment. They move from acting inward to core practice to acting out to embrace tools that connect you to the realm in which accomplishment for participants lives. In a nutshell, they are:

Chapter 6: Keep Your Program Live Longer: Describing programs to participants as having two parts is amazingly powerful. First, we need to offer you something useful. Second, you need to use it. You remain in our program while you use what you gained.

Chapter 7: Find the Sparkplugs. The best help can come from people and groups who live in the immediate setting of those in need and who will provide help without being paid to do so. Nonprofits are essential in making this happen.

Chapter 8: Try Something Else. Why did I not label this as an admonition to innovate? The reason is that the word suggests novelty and creativity. Innovation can best be seen as simply trying something new and seeing if it works. Innovation is not about what is new, but about what is better.

Chapter 9: Decrease Your Cost Per Gain. This means a change from distributing all costs over all participants, to loading costs on the participants who gain the results. This is the metric that puts cost and gain together.

Chapter 10: Move the Needle. Many donors are tired of success that amounts to drops in the bucket. They want to make a big dent. They are also willing to pay for it. Alas, most nonprofits cannot tell them what it would cost or how to achieve it.

PART III: takes us to the source of many practices that pull us away from results. It is our formats. These seemingly innocuous ways of shaping information have an outsized impact on how we think and act. I cover seven:

Chapter 11: The Organization Chart: From Boxes to the Spaces Between Them

Chapter 12: The Job Description: From Describing the Role to Defining its Achievement

Chapter 13: The Budget: From Money in Categories to Costs Accounted to Achievement

Chapter 14: The Resume: From Qualifications to Achievement Records

Chapter 15: The Strategic Plan: From Documents to Designs

Chapter 16: The Logic Model: From Theory to Informed Actions

Chapter 17: The Proposal: From Request to Investment Opportunity

In each format, a pivot is offered to a put results first. Job descriptions become result descriptions. Plans become designs. Logic becomes a way to predict what will be achieved.

PART IV: This covers two major new directions in philanthropy: collective action and diversity, equity, and inclusion (DEI). Both are at once fashionable and essential. Yet neither has fulfilled its promise, in part because the promise is stated as aspiration, rather than personal commitments people are prepared to make.

Chapter 18: Partnerships, Coalitions, Initiatives, Collaborations. This chapter considers collective action and impact, where the first problem is word mush. The various terms (collaboratives, networks, partnerships, coalitions, etc.) are used interchangeably. Results are to come out of the structures (such as steering committees) and processes (such as building agreement and trust). How we work together becomes a stronger focus than what we achieve together.

Chapter 19: Diversity, Equity, and Inclusion. It is now a leading topic in nonprofit conferences and magazines. Does a result framework apply to DEI? I think yes. It is not enough to have diversity, equity, and inclusion at the table. We have to use it to eliminate shameful disparities. While this takes national conversation, it also takes small projects with clear aiming points in every settlement in the nation. Putting results first matters.

PART V: Here is the action arm of the book. By that, I mean your action. I ask you to pick something—anything—that you found useful and find a way to take steps to apply it. One early step is finding some partners to help you. These "go-first" persons are actually more critical than the content for change. The best way to attract a go-first team is with the zest of a sparkplug. That can be you.

AFTERWARD: I suggest a compact between you and my group, Results 1st. We propose to stay at your side to help with examples, different tools—anything you need.

A few guidelines for using the book.

1. *This is not a novel and need not be read start to finish.* I do suggest reading Part I chapters in order before branching out. Parts II and III offer a menu of possibilities. You can implement something without going wide or even deep at the outset of change.

2. *Each chapter ends with Try It.* These are things you can do as an initial experience by yourself or with another person—most within an hour. All are doable in both large and small organizations. Results are an action, not a topic. At the same time they start with a different approach. Thinking differently is sure helpful in acting differently.

3. *The book is light on notes.* Most are added thoughts on how to look at something rather than a citation. You can readily Google to find virtually any group, person, or approach I reference. If you want page numbers for a document quoted, just ask us at **info@results1st.org**.

4. *When bringing in a book, article, or person, I consider its value, not its age.* Some ideas, approaches, or frameworks are 20 or more years old and remain highly relevant. Others grow obsolete within a year.

5. *The organization I created, Results 1st, has workbooks and templates for virtually all of the approaches described.* Just email us at **info@results1st.org** to tell us what you want to see. Priority in response goes to those who can tell us how they will use information we provide.

Finally, a hearty swig of the medicine preached. I cannot declare this book a success because of the number of copies it sells. Only you can make its impact possible by finding something of value and putting it to use. I hope you do.

HAL WILLIAMS
Bradenton, Florida
January 2024

PART I

Five Acts for Success

There's nothing remarkable about it. All one has to do is hit the right keys at the right time, and the instrument plays itself.

— Johann Sebastian Bach

If you do nothing, there will be no results.

— Mahatma Gandhi

High-achieving nonprofits do five things very well. They define, track, verify, improve, and communicate their results. Much of what most nonprofits do currently is not related to any of these. Your answers to five questions will put you squarely in a result mode:

* How do you define success, meaning results from your services?
* How do you know during a program if you need to make changes to be successful?
* How do you know which success was achieved?
* How do you improve your program with each cycle or use based on learning?
* How do you characterize what you achieve to attract more money and other help?

Let's act to answer them.

CHAPTER 1

Define Success and Set Targets

Two teachers, Jim and Susan, each request $500 to try a new approach they believe will reduce high absenteeism in their school. Jim pledges to do his best to solve a school-wide problem by working hard to attract students to all his classes. Susan states that she will focus on her second-period class, where, on average, 10 of 32 students are absent. She commits to reducing that from 10 to 5 students. In which teacher would you invest?

Susan is far more likely to produce a higher return. Why? Because she has a clear target on which to focus. Jim, in contrast, has no aiming point. He has no way of knowing when he is successful. This is the difference "putting results first" can make. People with clearly defined targets almost always outperform those who only pledge best effort.

Sadly, most outcome frameworks seem to drain the energy from personal and team commitments. Instead, they ask, "What are your measurable and quantitative objectives?" I have asked foundations using this expression what they see as the difference between "measurable" and "quantitative." Most have no clear distinction; they just say it sounds more comprehensive. I much prefer this question: How do you define success—meaning, the results from your services?

Activities vs. Results

In the list below, put an "A" on each item you would call an activity and an "R" if you would call it a result.

1. We will develop this new curriculum, which will be certified by the state.
2. Seventy percent of our participants say they really like our program.
3. Twenty more students will read at grade level.
4. Our resource directory will reach 5,000 people who need it.
5. We will greatly increase our number of mentors.
6. Forty students who have juvenile arrest records will commit no crimes over the next six months.
7. The state has invested an additional $200 million in high school education.
8. Our counselors have seen an additional 20 clients this year.

This is the distinction you must make to be result-centered. Items three and six are the only two in the list that should get the R. The rest are activities. The curriculum, no matter how conforming, says nothing about who gets better by using it. People saying they like something is not the same as them using it. What does "reaching" mean for the resource directory?

Many formats and habits we use steer us toward activities. In contracts, we see a "Scope of Services," not a "Scope of Results." Terms like "deliverables" speak to products like plans and curriculum that are of no use until participants apply them. On our websites, we get program activities and services on the front page. We have to go two to four clicks in to learn how many of those who were served benefitted.

In many instances, activities blossom into results as if by magic. From a publication on learning in New Jersey's colleges:

Based on Campus Compact's 2016 survey in New Jersey on member service, the average figure per campus for community-based learning courses taught at your member institutions was 73, while the average number of students attending these courses was 1,103. That is a remarkable number of people forging local commitments, networks, and skills necessary for today's employment opportunities.[1]

Wait a minute. How do we get from the activity of attending a course to forging local commitments? Results do not automatically spring from activities, especially when they are not stated in advance of the work.

Down the Result Trail

To get from activities to results, think of a progression that begins with activities. Start with some things you do for and with participants. Ask our favorite Results 1st question: So what? For example:

* We did the research to identify resources available in our community. So what?
* We put them into a resource manual and printed and distributed copies. So what?
* Some people said they read it and found it helpful. So what?
* Some people who read it said they connected with a resource they would not have known about without our work.

If you prefer, think of the trail as a set of "If/Then" connections. Take, for example, a project to get 50 people to visit a prenatal clinic and follow the advice given to them:

First, we will design, print, and mail brochures to 5,000 people who are pregnant or likely to become pregnant.

...And then? Some who get the brochure will choose to read it and call one of the clinics listed.

...And then? Some who call the clinic will both make and keep an appointment.

...And then? Some who visit the clinic will follow the nutritional and other advice given to them.

These approaches are simply ways to connect something to what happens next. Here's how this looks as a complete result trail from training and workshops:

Level 1: From Being There

1. *They came.* A program promised to have 40 people present, and it did.
2. *They liked it.* On the feedback form, 85% of attendees said they were satisfied or highly satisfied.
3. *They got it.* Participants could articulate what they found valuable from the program.

Level 2: From Early Application

4. *They remember.* Three weeks later, content has stuck with the attendees.
5. *They used it.* Participants report they applied something that had stuck with them.
6. *It worked!* What they tried made a tangible, positive difference.

Level 3: From What Sticks Longer Term

7. *They keep using what works.* The new behavior has become a routine practice.
8. *Other staff use the new practice.* The change has spread to other staff.

9. *Change is organization-wide.* Overall, gains are evident from the new practice.

Note that complete does not mean complex.

Just how far down the result trail do you need to go to declare victory? In the example just above, many workshops and other training materials declare success at Level 2. We had a good turnout, and 90% of participants said they were satisfied or highly satisfied with the program. As you can see from the remaining levels, this is just the beginning for results. The real gains are not even visible in most such programs.

One way to know when to stop is when you arrive at a result that can predict success. If a parent, caregiver, or child receives free books, this stops too short. We do not even know if they read the first page. If, however, a parent or caregiver reads with their child for 45 minutes at least five times a week and asks questions about what the story means, this activity is strongly connected with reading gains. Similarly, in health, exercising and eating fresh or frozen fruits and vegetables while avoiding high-sodium cans is equally correlated with managing chronic conditions like diabetes and hypertension. A term widely used now is Social Determinants of Health (SDOH). Food and financial security are just that—not just indicators, but determinants.

Results for Whom?

Is your program equally capable of helping all people who have the problem you address? The best nonprofits I know almost always say no. They have found that their approach is better able to help some people more than others. Most products and programs actually serve a niche, defined as the fit between approach and person. In an elementary school, for example, both a firm, directive approach as well as a more free-flowing, Montessori style can be effective approaches—for some students. I am always suspicious when a group tells me that their approach is so powerful that it works equally well for everyone who has the need they hope to address.

How well nonprofits know their participants is a critical factor in setting targets and knowing what to do to reach them. A colleague at the Freddie Mac Foundation included a proposal question that asked for a short description of two different participants—fictional names, but real people. In one proposal, they described a girl tempted to drop out of school because her parents were from a culture that put little value on educating females. My colleague then looked at the program description to see if they explicitly addressed this barrier—either by working with the family or producing stronger influences. They had not, and the program did not gain an investment.

One perspective that is helpful in looking at participant differences is the number and level of barriers faced. Here is an example from a prenatal health clinic whose desired result is babies who are healthy and in a normal weight range. Clients fell into three categories:

- Those with few barriers to desired result: no health insurance, no primary physician.
- Those with some barriers: no health insurance, no primary physician, first pregnancy, under 20 years old.
- Those with many barriers: no health insurance, no primary physician, first pregnancy, dropped out of school, single parent, smokes cigarettes, uses alcohol.

Barriers clearly inform program design. Persons with many barriers, for example, tend to need stronger intensity and longer duration of program. I worked with after-school programs, for example, that did not show great results until they separated those who came at least three times per week (the minimum needed to predict a gain) and those who came less.

Money needed also varies. Support to help a student two grade levels behind in reading is far more costly than the nudge needed to get a student already on the "bubble" for grade level reading. This difference can justify your higher costs. An added gain for your donors is that it gives them a way to see if you stick with the initial plan. They can verify that you do not shift during the program to only deal with those who have fewer challenges.

One practice that really helps understand participant similarities and differences is to treat them as a cohort. With a service mindset, the focus is meeting the numbers. As long as we initially have the 75 participants whom we said we would serve, it does not matter if some drop out and others come in. The cohort approach is different. It focuses on helping a defined group of participants get to the desired result. Dropouts and low-achieving participants remain in the count. As we will cover in Chapter 3, this also makes achievement easier to verify.

Target Practice

Great targets have six characteristics. I suggest you treat this as a checklist for how you define your aiming points.

#1: Reflect changes in behavior or conditions.

Which comes first, a change in attitude or behavior? I have no one answer but do know that to put results first, I need to have a way to know when those changes are achieved. I do know that If I focus on behaviors, I can more readily verify change. When the target is increased empowerment, self-esteem, or other vague conditions, it can be hard enough to define your goals, let alone articulate whether they are causes or effects. Beware of assumptions that sound good but may have it wrong. One such assumption is that students with higher self-esteem get better grades in school. Therefore, we should focus on building self-esteem. Most studies show the causal arrow goes either way. Self-esteem does not generally cause academic achievement. Achievement causes self-esteem.[2]

One question helps to get from a condition or attitude to a behavior: What is it that a person with higher self-esteem, empowerment, collaborative inclination, or anything else can do that one with a lower level of those traits cannot? A midwestern nonprofit with which I worked had a great answer. They defined empowerment as having and making choices. Success meant that they could tell you of at least two options and had a reason for picking one over the other. I loved this and have many more examples.

#2: Set goals relative to what would have happened without the program.
We think of a baseline as meaning the place where participants are before the program starts. In a result framework, an equally critical baseline is where the participants would be if the program did not exist. A school, for example, might set a target of getting another 50 students to grade level in reading next year—a 10% gain over last year. Until we know the trend line for the past three years, we do not know how to set that level. If the school has been trending upwards by 10% a year for the last three years, the target level of 10% is no more than what would be presumed to happen without a new program. On the other hand, if the trend were a 10% decrease in reading, the 10% gain is actually a 20% gain over what would have happened without the program.

The trendline focus is also used by your investors. I worked with a foundation in North Carolina inclined to focus on reducing teen pregnancy. In that area, teen pregnancy was already dropping by some 15% per year. The foundation chose to refocus on housing, where the rate of homelessness was rising by about that same amount per year.

#3: Include numbers, not just percentages.

If 80% of your 200 participants achieved a result, that's 160 people who have benefitted. If you started with five, it means four. Similarly, if I say that we helped 200 people, that's very impressive if we started with 220 participants and not impressive if we started with 1,000. In the first case, it is 90% who gained. In the second it is only 20%. Numbers and percentages need each other to make contextual sense.

Numbers, in my experience, are more personal. Each reflects a person. Legendary school district turnaround leader Tony Amato came into Hartford, CT, which had, for some time, ranked last in student achievement among the urban areas in Connecticut. He proclaimed that Hartford would never be last again. When he told each principal that they must get 10% more students to grade level to get out of the cellar, most said that was not possible. He then noted that this meant that each teacher needed to get just two more students to read at level. With that shift in how the goal was presented, virtually all teachers said they could—and did.

Numbers are best set as minimums, not as ranges. If you say the target is 20 to 30 people getting to a desired gain, the high end is 50% higher than the low end. Ranges are not aiming points. Targets speak to the minimal number that must achieve to declare success.

Numbers are a good provision to have for broader reasons. My friend, Mike Marvin, co-founder of MapInfo, once observed that he looks for leaders in both for-profit and nonprofit organizations who have some numerical anchors. Since hearing that gem, I ask nonprofit leaders and staff for a number. How many participants are in your program? How many came last week? What was your revenue last year? What is your budget for this year? People with vague or no answers will say they can look it up, and some even make it a point of pride that they do not jam their heads with such trivia. Mike's point was—and is—that numbers let you think about what to change in a way that narratives alone do not.

#4: Include a needed threshold of improvement.

Saying that something good will go up or something bad will go down is of little value. An increase in grade average from 2.0 to 2.1, for example, may well not be enough to influence graduation rates. The question is what minimal gain is needed to make a real difference. Eating two to three helpings of fresh fruits and vegetables a week is not enough to forecast better health. That could take at least five times per week. Note that the target should be set for the number of persons who reached a specific threshold. This also goes deeper than a metric of average gain. If a program has one person make a great gain and seven more who made gains not large enough to matter, relying on averages would show that I hit moderate gains for eight persons. In reality, only one reached the minimum gain needed to forecast success.

The best targets reflect a threshold that has needed breakout. If a school proudly says that a student two grade levels behind will, for the first time, make a year's growth in a year's time, that student will always be two years behind.

#5: Create a strategy with ambitious, but reachable goals.

Small increments of improvement are typically not exciting. Major intended gains galvanize energy and attention. The great organizational thought leader Jim Collins coined the term BHAG—a Bit Hairy, Audacious Goal.[3] If a group wants to improve something by as little as five or even 10%, they are likely to think they can do that by simply redoubling efforts. If they want to get to 50%, they know they need a different strategy.

Targets are expectations, and the level at which they are set influences achievement. Research in education, for example, shows that when teachers are told that specific students have great potential to perform at unexpectedly high levels, they often do so. Prophecies can be self-fulfilling. I see this in many nonprofits where their participants really struggle. Acceptance of an undesired condition is not a good starting point.

At the same time, impossibly high targets are equally misguided. They can lead to the explanation that a group aimed for the stars but always knew their intended results were aspirational. I often see this with the statement that 100% of participants will get to gain. In most programs, not everyone will achieve success for a variety of reasons the nonprofits cannot overcome. Set your target within the realm of possibility.

Costs enter the picture of how high to aim. I once guided a series of public hearings on ground water pollution for the EPA. The money needed to get the last 2% of a pollutant out of surface water, in one case, was more than it took to remove the first 98%. Does this mean we abandon the 2 out of 100 students who cannot get to grade-level reading with our program? Of course not. It does mean we may need to fit them with a different program that is highly realistic about what it will take.

#6: Include everyone who can help achieve your goal.

My daughter, Gillian, during her School Turnaround program, told me of the people who work in her cafeteria. Rather than continuing to ask students if they wanted peas or beans, the cafeteria workers started asking students what book they had read last night. When the next set of grades came out and the school had greatly increased their reading scores, who felt they deserved some credit? The cafeteria workers. And they did. Most custodians do not see any connection between cleaning bathrooms and improvements in reading levels. In one instance, I saw janitors form relationships with struggling students and spend 20 minutes each day helping them.

In another, I saw a project teach illiterate grandparents the 25 words they needed to know to read a story with children. Targets need ways to let people in. This requires that everyone involved can see a way in which they can help.

Beyond knowing how to help, people need confidence that the target can be hit. I worked with a Florida elementary school with well under half the students reading at grade level. The principal set a target of getting from almost 75% reading below grade level to 75% reading at grade level in three years. The target was 10x4x3. Get 10 more students on grade level in four grades for three years. The principal had a sheet which showed the year-by-year changes needed to achieve this.

No one has a higher stake in hitting the target than the participant. Ironically, they are often seen in passive terms of getting help. In my experience, programs where the participants not only understand and agree with a target, but co-own it, are the most successful. One good approach is to set targets in front of the participants. Here are examples of participants who took ownership of their neighborhood youth program involving at-risk students in Seattle, and tried to pass it on to others:

- I now boost positive energy in myself and others. Here are two persons who can verify that.
- I have played a key role in implementing a neighborhood project. Here is an example.
- I can define the value of what I bring to employers. Got two minutes? Let me show you.
- I have avoided involvement in any crime!

Many groups can follow this path, including colleges with their course descriptions. Most are written to say what will be taught and what the student will know. "The student will gain an understanding of this and a way to apply it in their thinking." I worked with faculty at Emory and Henry College to change this to the student view: "After the course, this is what I will know, and these are the new skills I will have so I can put that knowledge to use."

Students and other customers of products and services gain power by knowing what they want. My colleague, Susie Bowie, speaks to going into a store to get her iPhone fixed after drowning it while kayaking. She appreciated the friendly associate with lots of personality and the great effort they made to set an environment for a rich experience. But when she walked out, the only thing that mattered was that her phone worked. This has some applicability to some nonprofit programs where the participant just wants to get the result for which they came.

Results for Systemic Change

While most nonprofit programs focus on helping individuals and families, some target systemic factors which put severe limits on personal accomplishment. Some conditions are literal structures, like grocery stores in a food desert or a clinic in a remote area. Other changes are less visible. Laws and practices that influence resource distribution, health, justice, education achievement, and comparative justice involve broad and deep factors beyond the ability of the nonprofit to directly influence. Most results in this area look to address inequities disproportionately faced by persons of color. We will cover this in much more detail in Chapter 19. Work on systemic results is often labeled as advocacy and is intended to defend rights as much as meet needs.

I do think it is possible and highly useful to set targets for programs addressing structural or systemic changes. It is always possible to define work in a way that ensures you know progress is being made. With specific structures, this part is easy: count the people using facilities that are presumed to provide further access. The focus is not on proximity to the resource, but on its use.

When it comes to major decisions on money and policy, the starting point is defining decision makers and a progression of their getting stuff, reading it, and reporting it helps them to see a full picture. If a group is trying to get a bill or policy passed by a county commission with 12 members, for example, an initial accomplishment may be to get at least eight of them to acknowledge that they have received and read the nonprofit's materials and think some of the points deserve consideration. The starting point is moving from building awareness among thousands to focussing on a much lower number of individuals whose actions are needed to make something happen. Chunking it down can also turn up small victories sooner. A group may not be able to change capital markets in a city but prove successful at getting one bank to make available $250,000 in loans to underrepresented groups with solid business plans.

Know the Finish Line While at the Starting Line

Can you imagine a runner in the starting blocks not knowing if the finish line was a quarter mile or a mile away? That can happen with nonprofit programs where direction is clear but the end goal is not. Traditional structures and processes of program planning are so ingrained that they can take over without you even knowing it. Here are the two concerns I hear about why results cannot be set at the outset of programs:

Concern #1: We lack a baseline.

We need to postpone creating targets until more data are available on participant problems and current level of achievement. Sure, there is always room for more data before acting. The best way to generate information, however, is to start with what you have and set a target high enough that it is clearly beyond current performance. At that point, I am not sure the exact aiming point matters. People with targets outperform those waiting for precisions to set them. Motion is the best path to success in many cases.[4]

Concern #2: We need widespread agreement before we act. Listening tours, studies, surveys, and other activities to define needs generally end with the same conclusions. Most people want to live in a safe house, have enough money to cover their expenses, manage chronic health conditions, and see their kids achieve in school. Most want to feel secure and happy. Indeed, far fewer persons in need call for more analysis than do the nonprofits which serve them.

When results are based on agreement, the focus is on a group already assembled. If, however, a leader says that they are looking for people and groups to join them in achieving a specific gain, the door is open to any group attracted by that aiming point.

Another form of failure to launch comes within organizations where units or departments say they cannot act until they get direction. Yes they can. Just ask your bosses if you can start to work toward a target you have set. Even weak leaders won't try to keep you from improving until you hear further from them. Targets can thrive with fuzziness at the top.

When Targets are Elusive

I keep hearing from groups that, in their domain, it is just not possible to set clear results. My view is that every program and pursuit can do so by following two guidelines. First, start by characterizing the gain sought. Metrics come after that. Second, ask if the group believes that some groups in their field achieve more gain than do others. If the answer is yes—and it usually is—you have a way in. To define better or worse, there has to be some standard the respondent is using. Start there.

Let's take a look at three areas: prevention, essential human services, and the arts.

1. Prevention

How can you measure that which did not happen? You can! If I want to prevent at-risk students from getting juvenile justice convictions, I can ask how many, in the population I serve, tend to get convicted each year. I can compare that with how many participants do so in the year after our program.

An example: I worked with a large foundation in New York City that supports teen pregnancy prevention. The foundation asked me to work with nonprofits who had previously told funders how many workshops they held and how much the at-risk young people liked the workshops. "Not sufficient," said my client as they shifted from only funding programs to investing in results. We want to know the effect on teen pregnancy rates in the South Bronx.

One nonprofit handled this very well. It narrowed its focus to two middle schools and indicated it would work with twenty at-risk young students in each. Staff asked three persons, including the guidance counselor, a teacher, and an after-school enrichment aide, to independently assess the students and determine how many were likely to get pregnant within the next 18 months. Given that the response was an aggregate for the group of 20, this was not seen as violating confidentiality. The responses were all close to 25%, which would mean five unplanned pregnancies. They set their target of no more than two and noted that this would mean about three pregnancies prevented. "About" is not perfect, but it is far more than a guess or a hope.

Another approach is to use risk factors known to influence achievement. Child neglect and abuse are among the many fields where getting persons out of a high-risk category is shown to mean less problem incidence. You can reasonably rely on research statistics to forecast how many abuses or other problem instances you have prevented.

2. Essential Human Services

Some nonprofits deal with those who struggle with the basics of life. They face abject poverty, despair, illiteracy, mental health impairment, and/or other conditions. Their logic is that people are hungry, so they feed them. The meal is the gain. Begin there. Yes—whether it is breakfast, a hot shower, a washing machine, a bus voucher, or something else, direct help is the critical starting point. As Abrahman Maslow put it in his famous hierarchy of needs, it is hard to work on self-actualization when your roof leaks. When the service is the result, at least some aspects of progress can become measurable right away. Those include:

* Cost per person. Does it go up or down with volume?
* Waiting lines. Changes over time in the number of people needing the service.
* Quality of products served. Is the meal healthy, or just plentiful?
* Participant experience. What participants see as the gain and how they were treated and feel about it.

All of these can become targets. The differences in efficiency and cost, if nothing else, is of great interest to philanthropy.

Another distinction that is increasingly important to some investors in nonprofit programs is if you can get some people out of that line for your service and help them become more self-sufficient. I have worked with several nonprofits in different states who effectively use their basic service to identify people who, with help, can reach a point where they no longer need the help. With homelessness, these are often persons who simply lack the upfront money needed for a home—in some cases, even with a job. My guess is that your direct service or care staff have always seen major differences between the people ready and able to take the step toward independence and those who are not.

3. The Arts

Who is to say if a work of art is good or bad? I have two answers: the intended audience and the artists. I like this framework for getting to accomplishment:

* Who came? We can count:
  * The number attending vs. projections
  * The mix of those attending in terms of location and income
  * Those coming for the first time
* How many gained something? We can count:
  * The number who say they are very glad they came
  * Those who can tell you one aspect or piece they really enjoyed
  * The proportion of those attending for the first time who say they will come again
* How did this enrich our nonprofit? We can count:
  * If our audience is diversifying from its beginnings
  * Revenue and the share of cost that ticket revenue covers

- Those living nearby who say it builds neighborhood strength

Artistic intentions need different results. Large orchestras strive for world-class performance standards. Community orchestras seek to provide enrichment and social connection. Each can find its stride with something they want to improve.

My colleague, the CEO of Results 1st, worked with an impressive nonprofit that runs a performing arts center in Bradenton, Florida. They wanted to improve their impact on the lives of the audience members as well as the cast by seeking out and helping with any accommodations they needed to enjoy the performances. They set targets for the first quarter of 2022, and at the end, reported these results:

- Of the 77 actors cast, seven needed and received accommodations and reported that they could perform at their best.
- Of the 5,940 patrons, a total of 81 persons responded to our new invitation to say they needed special accommodations for listening, low vision, seating space, or other needs. All were accommodated.

To date, this discussion has stayed clear of artistic merit. That, presumably, is handled by juried exhibitions and expert reviews. While some see this as independent of size or appreciation of the audience, I see a strong connection. Most Broadway shows close rather quickly. The audience has spoken. In other cases, such as the third-grade holiday show or elementary band performance, enthusiasm and nurturing are independent of how well the piece was written, drawn, or performed.

Achievement as the Constant

In a surprising number of cases, if a program seems in danger of not achieving its intended results, the ends, rather than the means, are modified! If Jim's humanistic approach to education is not leading to increased engagement, it is planting seeds for longer-term change. If no one calls the 800-Number for help, it must be that the advice in the public service message is self-explanatory. If people in a job-training program do not get and keep jobs, the real gain is that they have a higher sense of self-esteem. Hold the activity constant and let the results vary.

With Results 1st, the priorities are reversed. The desired change stays constant, and activities are allowed to vary. Consider a Yonkers high school with which I worked, where students were required to recite a key passage from the Bill of Rights. A teacher indicated that the reason 60% of his students were in danger of failing his course was that they could not or would not memorize it. He believed a humanistic approach, including role playing the Founding Fathers, would lead to at least 20 of his students passing the test. One week into his two-week initiative, the teacher saw virtually no change. The teacher awakened early one morning to a startling realization: the students did have the ability to memorize the assignment perfectly—if it was on their terms. In class that day, he told the students that he wanted them to rap the Bill of Rights. They could form groups and use music and instruments. The only rule was that they must use the exact words in an exact order. Almost all of the students learned the required passage—and had a greater sense of its meaning.

TRY IT

1. Look at a few key materials used to describe your organization and its programs. Make a list of the most critical definers that define an activity and a list of those that

speak to a result. Take one important activity on your list and recast it in terms of what you achieve.

2. Consider a program where the specific level of gain is either not stated or without a clear rationale. Define a threshold for gain that reflects the minimum level of change you and your colleagues see as needed to make a difference.

CHAPTER 2

Track to Success

Six months ago, you gave me my first $500,000 to start this business. I am pleased to report that I spent all the money in a responsible and legal way. I found office space, hired people, added great new features to my product, engaged an ad agency, and developed a strategic plan. My expense documentation is excellent, and my reports were all submitted on time. I am ready for my second $500,000.

The investors getting this news are not reassured. They want to know if you have found early customers and learned what it will take to sell them on your product. Nonprofits face a similar situation. Their donors want to know, at midpoint, if you are on track for the promised results with the time and money remaining. How about this answer? We are halfway through the program year, have spent half the money, and are on schedule with our workplan. Smart donors are not impressed. You can get all the way through your workplan and spend all the money only to find that participants do not get the gain you are seeking. This chapter introduces you to milestones, a powerful tool that not only lets you know when you are off course, but suggests what to do when you are.

A milestone, in its simplest definition, is whatever tells you that your participants are on track to achieve the intended result. This term is often seen as interchangeable with indicators and benchmarks. It is not. Indicators are often used as a surrogate where the result, and progress toward it, are presumed not visible. Benchmarks are most often used to show deliverables, often within a project management framework. In both cases, they are more likely than not to focus on what the nonprofit does rather than what the participants get. The real sort is your mindset. Indicators and benchmarks are typically seen as noting achievements to date. Milestones focus on what comes next and how to get there.

Much of the rigor in a result framework is grounded in prediction. Does achievement on this assessment or that risk factor predict the result you seek? The best predictors are those that prove accurate.

From Workplan to Milestones

Change is often easier when you start with what you do now. I worked with a job program that had a budget of $100,000, whose leaders said they would get 40 people a living-wage job that they would keep for six months. These were their first four workplan steps:

1. Prepare and mail program announcement
2. Respond to phone calls and emails
3. Hold an in-person info session
4. Enroll participants

The last step is the first milestone: enrollment. The wording becomes critical. The milestone is not what you do to enroll participants, but what they do that makes them show up. Milestones take you deeper as you see the world through the eyes of potential, and then actual, participants. Here is an example, used by my colleague, Cheri Coryea, from a food-security program.

This agreement, between Jack Pepper and Village Health, is our commitment to each other to achieve the result of her longer and happier life.

Village Health commits to:

- Secure Jack access, at no or low cost, to fresh and/or frozen fruits and vegetables.
- Provide the means needed for Jack to cook healthy foods—a countertop stove, microwave, etc.
- Operate within the time Jack has available to get and cook food.

Jack commits to:

- Prepare, cook, and eat these healthy foods five times weekly, at minimum.
- Participate in all sessions, including diary entries and all check-ins.
- Stick to this program for the three months needed to show a difference in health.

I would prefer to get 20 persons to sign the agreement than 60 persons to only enroll by giving their name and number. Let's keep going with the job example. The next five workplan steps in this jobs program were:

- Finalize curriculum and hire instructors
- Hold all sessions
- Pair job coaches with participants
- Place participants with potential employers for a trial period
- Job coaches make three site visits to support participants

This continues to say what the program does. We traded in these five steps for three milestones that predicted participants getting and keeping a living-wage job:

- At the end of the first session, participants want to return and can say what they learned that will help them get and keep a job.

* At the end of training, participants show high engagement, knowledge, and confidence in getting and keeping a job.

* After the two-week trial period, the participant and their employer or supervisor report that the participant shows very good promise and will be offered a full-time job.

Here's the full picture:

Workplan Steps
1. Prepare and mail program announcement
2. Respond to phone calls and emails
3. Hold in-person info sessions
4. Enroll participants
5. Finalize curriculum and hire instructors and mentors
6. Hold all sessions
7. Pair mentors with participants
8. Place participants with employers for trial period
9. Make three site visits to monitor and support

Milestones
1. Participants commit
2. Participants attend first session and want to continue
3. At the end of training, participants have the skills, confidence, and knowledge to get and keep a job
4. After the two-week trial period, participants and employers forecast that the job will last

Note that there is not a one-to-one correspondence between workplan and milestones. In this case, steps one through four all contribute to milestone one. In general, milestone lists are much shorter than worklan steps.

A good approach would be to start with the workplan steps and ask of each what has to happen for participants. You hold all sessions. So what? What do we need to see and hear from participants after the final session that tells you they are on track for success?

Conversion Ratios

Milestones let you know if, at each point in the program, you have enough people to hit your target. For programs with about 30 or more participants, I suggest you start by assuming 100 participants for easy computations. You can then apply percentages for your actual starting number. For small programs, start with 10. I call this the conversion ratio—how many participants convert from one milestone accomplishment to the next. What is your best guess as to how many who enroll will show up? And how many who come to the first session will come to the remaining five? In the jobs example, the group projected the following numbers:

MILESTONE	NUMBER
1. Participants commit.	100
2. Participants attend the first session and can name what they learned.	85
3. Participants attend all sessions and demonstrate needed skills and confidence.	50
4. After the two-week trial employment period, participants and employers forecast that the job will last.	45
Result: 40 jobs retained for six months	

Without this roadmap, a nonprofit might be pleased with 60 participants completing the second milestone in this example, noting that they have 45 more progressing than needed for the result. By their own conversion logic, they are behind.

Projecting and tracking numbers is also invaluable in knowing where to make program improvements. In the above chart, by far the biggest fallout occurs after the first session. This is where change will make a difference. The first step is to figure out what is happening. Variation among kinds of persons moving forward or not is high. At the group level, differences may be race, age, gender, or something else. Or, there could be personal factors creating variation that relate to staff more than participants. If the participants with one job coach are keeping their jobs while participants with another job coach are not, that is a good indicator of who will proceed.

Here's the good news: if you can improve your conversion ratios, you do not need more people. You just need to make the program work better for those already in it. This is also efficient in that you soon know these persons individually. Starting with a fresh supply of participants means that knowledge development must start over. More importantly, it avoids the disappointment and loss of confidence from dropping out. With higher numbers achieving, you also need less effort in the beginning. In the encyclopedia example, great salespersons could pre-qualify customers such that they get one in five to agree to use the product, and they were so persuasive that they also got one in five to buy. Those people do not need to start with 100 participants. They could start with 25.

Adding Time and Money

If I am your financial advisor and tell you I made 12% on your money, you would want to know if I did that over one year or three.

Time matters equally in nonprofit programs. While a no-cost contract extension sounds neutral and acceptable, it is not. On the one hand, it does harm to participants. It may mean that a student must repeat a grade because the help needed was not timely. Or, a person may not get the fresh fruits and vegetables needed to lower blood pressure or blood sugar in time to prevent real harm. Few people find their problems mitigated by waiting.

Delays also create hardship for the organization. Most programs are paying staff and other expenses during the delay period. While they may do so by dipping into the project budget, they will then run out of money before the project ends. Also, costs may rise, and opportunities for in-kind or other contributions disappear. Most opportunities are time-bound.

Think of it this way: Group A has 40 persons in a six-month program cycle to earn an important gain. This is 240 persons benefiting in three years. Group B runs one month late each cycle and achieves the same result. Their total for three years is 200 persons benefiting.

Let's now bring in costs. Traditionally, money is tracked by a budget. If we are spending within numbers projected, we are on track. With milestones, the question shifts to what you can afford to spend to get the numbers projected. A good approach is to look at a budget and apportion time and other expenses to milestones. A better approach is to build the budget by what it will take for each milestone and then add it up. I find that approaching total costs in this way frequently leads to a very different number than overall budgeting. Either way, you are tracking money spent by each milestone to know if you have enough money left for remaining ones.

Let's add time and costs to the jobs example and portray this as what it is: a funnel.

MILESTONE	NUMBER	DATE	COST
Participants commit.	100	MAY 1	5,000
Participants attend the first session and can name what they learned.	85	JUNE 15	20,000
Participants attend all sessions and demonstrate needed just skills and confidence.	50	SEPTEMBER 1	30,000
After two weeks of trial employment period, participants and employers forecast the job will last.	45	SEPTEMBER 30	15,000
Results: 40 Jobs retained 6 months			

Numbers, time, and money come together in milestone tracking. If conversion ratios lead to fewer persons progressing, you may not be able to hit your target. If delays occur, you will also incur more costs. If you run short on money, the organization may not be able to keep up the program. If you do not have fallout and all participants stay with you, a visual image is still important. I like pipelines or other depictions of flow. Presumably, some participants swim or float faster than others.

Participant Progression

In many fields, research and experience suggest stages or steps of participant progress toward a result. An example is fundraising, where a typical set of categories used by a development staff looks like this:

Cold: The person is in a group (eg, alumni) and presumed to be interested. (500)

Cool: The person once came to an event or gave $25. Some sign of interest. (20)

Warm: The prospect chooses to have some interaction with people or information. Warmer still is taking some initiative—asking questions, doing a site visit, requesting materials. (6)

Hot: They make a first gift. (3)

Sizzling: They increase and repeat their gift two more times. (1)

What can I get from this? First, I would probably not bother with cold. On the one hand, it is so discouraging to go from 200 to 1. Getting 1 in 20 sounds more doable. Second, I would focus on increasing conversion from cool to warm. This is where my fall-off is. We can get to such insights by starting with what is known about the progression of donors.

I use a fundraising progression, since it is often tracked carefully in software. I wrote a series of blog entries for the Huffington Post with Marc Chardin, then CEO of Blackbaud, in which we mused on why organizations failed to use the same discipline to track their participants that they use to track donors. As with contributors, a few milestones hold for many programs. One is engagement. The participant who actively connects with a program, its presenters, and/or other participants is much more likely to gain than one who is simply present. The second is intentionality. The participant whose present behavior is purposeful toward achieving something is far more likely to use your program than a person who is drifting. Can you see and hear engagement and intentionality? Sure. That's next.

I'm Here for the Donuts

Ask every participant walking through the door of a community center on a Saturday morning why they are there. Their responses fall into two categories: either, I'm here to get to the second floor to learn how to write a resume, or I'm here for the donuts. I repeatedly find that the right simple questions can get you great insight.

On engagement, I ask my clients if they can tell when a person is engaged or not. They say yes. They speak to how those engaged lift their eyes to something in the room and show immediate reactions to what they see and hear. They see more smiles, fewer frowns. Some observant staff also speak to progression. Some may begin clearly with little or no engagement. They are present but seem elsewhere. Then comes an occasional gleam or grin. Then movement, as the participant responds quickly rather than waiting to be asked. Then, they see participants take initiative, moving from reacting promptly to acting first.

Do not worry if what you observe is not research-based or proven. Any changes in a person that can forecast if they are embracing and using a program is helpful. Let others worry about making it work in theory.

Participants Coming and Going

Here's a news flash: nonprofit programs do not generally fit the tidy timeline of a grant period. They do not begin with all participants starting on January 1 and earning their gain on December 31. They may well stream in throughout the year. Further participants take different durations to get to the gain. As if this is not enough, they may well start in one program year and finish in the next. How do we track and report given these challenges?

The best approach, in my view, is to start with the cycle time of individual participants. From their day of entry, how long do you forecast it will take most to get to the gain? Use your times set on milestones to answer that. Now forecast the number of new participants that will enter your program each month. Simple software can then tell you how many will achieve the result each month based on that time. Where you have great variation, break out two or three groupings which project different time lengths. For example, in a financial security program meant to help participants save $500 for use in unexpected expenses, groupings may be:

- About 25% of our participants can do this within three months. They have a job and just need to spend differently.
- About 25% of our participants can do this in six months. They have the desire but also have some fixed costs that make savings come more slowly.
- About 50% of participants will need a full year. Like many of us, they find it very difficult to save given impulses or other drivers to buy beyond budgets.

The average length from entry to result for the three categories above is eight months. So, your start is projecting that eight months after each person enters, they will, on average, leave with the result. Your first refinement is immediate. Lower this number by your falloff shown in conversion ratios. If 50% of those who start get to the finish line, drop the starting number in half to show how many should show as completing eight months after they begin. Whew—this sounds complicated as I write it. Just email Results 1st, and we will talk with you about Target Track software that does the math for you—and us.

Organizational Milestones

While most milestones reflect participant progress, some concentrate on what the organization needs to put in place. I often suggest elevating hiring from an activity to a milestone, for example, because it is so often a source of delay. How often is a program pushed back because a program leader or key staff person is not yet in place? It took two weeks longer than anticipated to post the job. The person chosen dropped out. No qualified applicants applied for the money offered. We had a delay getting everyone to meet the finalists. An employment agreement took two extra weeks for our attorney to finalize. Whatever the reasons, a two-month hiring period becomes four months—or longer. Knowing this, why do so many nonprofits do so little to start hiring at a much earlier moment? My answer is that they did not make this a milestone.

Once an activity is elevated to milestone level, we also look at what it produces more carefully. Yes, we hired a person with a master's degree and five years of experience. Did they, however, have the energy and skills to fire up staff and participants? This also applies to curricula, software, a specialized van, or anything else. I have seen tracking systems selected, for example, that arrive in a timely way but without the features needed for success. The curricula that looked great on PowerPoint showed huge flaws on information retention when first put to use. Our tools are all in English, and half of our participants can't speak or read it. Stating what must be included in the person or system to forecast success is critical in the area of organizational requirements.

In general, organizational milestones come early. They are the essential setup for a project to succeed. Milestones that test assumptions are the most important early focus when it is time to make changes. An example of a milestone that should have been:

A year was spent designing a program for homeless females with kids to move upstate from New York City. It was then implemented by retrofitting a large building in upstate New York to create apartments for females and children to occupy while participating in a job training program. Millions of dollars were spent and the doors opened. Few came. They assumed that because the program was "tailored to their needs," females with kids would rush to it, but that did not hold up.

While the mothers and caregivers felt homeless, their kids were rooted in schools and local activities and did not want to leave. The program should have tested the concept with a two-unit apartment rented for one month to find the possible roadblocks to their plan.

Other assumptions are about money needed. Program costs are rarely tested by nonprofits as carefully as they should be, and the budget may prove off by not just 5%, but sometimes 50%. A New York City nonprofit, for example, built and funded its budget for home visits on the assumption that a staff person could make six visits a day. They discovered too late that the staff time spent on changing appointments and slow subways reduced the reality to an average of three daily visits. Early learnings about productivity and many other matters can be tested, especially by accelerating them to the earliest possible point. That comes next.

Accelerating Intervention

My colleague, Les Loomis, a highly successful principal and superintendent, knew that the best predictor of failure to graduate high school was course failure in grades 9 and 10. Traditionally, the first benchmark assessment of the year comes in one or two months. Les wanted to know who was falling behind earlier. He asked teachers in his client district schools when they first knew that a student was in danger of failing their course. Teachers replied that they can tell in one to three weeks. What do you look at? Engagement, they said. It is not enough for a student to sit there politely. They have to have some interaction—whether with the teacher, other students, or the content.

This finding led Les and teachers to define the milestone of student engagement with a date of just one or two weeks into the start of the school year. They then put in place steps to build engagement using a pyramid of interventions. The first action with a student who was not engaged with the course was for the teacher to speak with the student to see what was going on. More extensive interventions follow if the changes made are not enough.

Milestones set for an early point are far more powerful than when positioned later. This principle is widely used with commercial products. When a paint manufacturer wants to know how its new formula will stand the test of time, it does not wait five years to see what happens. Rather, it exposes the painted surface to intensive heat, cold, humidity, and other key factors in a very compressed time. Rapid acceleration is equally useful with nonprofit programs.

Milestone management has one requirement: the belief that you can do something better. It is always tempting to say that nothing is wrong with the program. It is the weather, the government, the local economy, a busy time of year, or another external factor that is causing delays. In education, I have heard principals and teachers say that course failure is higher this year because it is a "slow class." The best schools will believe that they are the problem, not the students. They have not yet figured out how to help some students move forward.

Milestone tracking can prompt changes on the spot. I was challenged to do that in Glasgow, Scotland, where I was working with some 25 persons in local housing associations to figure out ways to increase houses for low-income residents. I began by sharing my target: of the 25 of you here today, at least 18 of you will leave the workshop with an innovative housing approach you are committed to trying. I had a milestone of "12x12.". I needed my first 12 persons by noon, which was two hours into a six-hour program. If I divided the 18 persons needed by six hours, I would have a milestone of three persons per hour, or six by lunch. Rarely does such linear thinking define milestone numbers. The first two hours were my best stuff, and their freshest receptivity. Just before lunch, I did my milestone check-in. "How many of you would say that you have identified an innovation you want to try? I saw eight hands. I was off the needed pace. Further, I could see some frozen faces and heads shaking. I had to take action. "For those of you who have not found an innovation yet, I must ask why. What could I do this afternoon to help you find an innovation to pursue?"

I turn to one of the head shakers and ask why I am not connecting with him. "Well, Hal, I'll tell you why you are not 'connecting' with me," he said. "You have crossed the pond with many examples from the U.S., which do not resonate for us. And where you have tried to fit in by using some UK examples, your examples are from England. This is Scotland." Oops.

The rest of my PowerPoint was not just irrelevant, but harmful. I had to change my approach immediately. I noted that I did not have Scottish examples of innovations but would bet that some participants did. I looked at a few people who were really engaged and asked if they could provide local examples. They agreed, and I achieved my 18-person target.

Taking immediate action, however, does require rapid diagnosis. In many programs, for example, it is critical to know if the participant challenge is motivation or capability. Interventions will vary greatly. Another distinction is between fit to the program and fit to the person delivering it. Some participants get the content but don't feel encouraged or supported by the persons to whom they relate. In other cases, that relationship is great, but the content does not seem applicable or understandable.

Diagnosis tells you which option is likely to work best. One choice is between changing the program or its environment. My daughter, Jessica, is a school psychologist supporting students with disabilities. She finds the simple step of rearranging the classroom can have an effect on disruptive behaviors. She points to the environmental cues and triggers for behaviors that are often surprisingly local. There is "furniture" in all programs, including spaces and layouts for participants who might find the setting itself as a barrier. I find this with meeting spaces. Hollow squares with long sides make it impossible for people to really interact, and theater or classroom style scream passivity. Gordon Townsend, then CEO of Avis Rent-a-Car, took out the chairs for all of his meetings. He reports that sessions were shorter and sharper.[5]

Starting Simple

Smaller nonprofits may feel that they can't afford the cost or the time to do serious tracking. They can, because the chances are excellent that their problem is not software. Our Results 1st CEO introduced a very simple spreadsheet she called "The Tracker." It allowed for entering names and dates of completion for each milestone and target. My first reaction was to say this is too simple. My second was to watch many nonprofits use it to clear advantage. They listed names and dates of participants at entry and added updates when they hit milestones. Unlike scattered case notes or files, everything showing progress for a participant was on one page.

The Tracker is in Excel to enhance the calculations on numbers of participants at milestones but can also be done in a simple Word format. If you are more advanced and use client management software, just make sure you can pull up progress points that matter. I see some formats where many procedural steps that are not related to achievement are included. Also, make sure you can manage by exception—ie, get lists of participants who have not hit a milestone within a week of projection.

Most existing systems for tracking have two highly distinct kinds of data: checklists for activities and progress and case notes and observations. These remain separate. When a system says it accommodates case notes, it simply means it provides a way to enter them in the same software. It is much stronger to find a simple way to connect case notes to milestones by placing them adjacent to numbers. Rather than simply noting that this is what you see at the fourth visit, it is more valuable to see the time the participant either achieves a milestone or is clearly falling behind. Notes can include what, if anything, needs to be done to help a participant for whom the program is not working. Again, this is not complicated once your notes focus on explaining progress or its lack.

TRY IT

1. Identify a participant you can contact who dropped out of one of your programs. Ask them why. Discuss what you might have done to keep and help them–or get them to a different program. Then ask yourself if you could have known earlier that they were falling behind and what that milestone would be.

2. Make up a simple tracking sheet for any of your programs and put the first 10 names in a column on the left. Then add three columns that tell you what you most want to check off–with dates–to show participants are on track to reach the target.

CHAPTER 3

Verify Achievement

Your program has ended, and the donor wants to know if it was successful. You could say:

* This was a great program. Here is a summary of the exciting activities with media coverage showing how much the young students enjoyed it.
* Ninety percent of the students and 75% of their parents said they were satisfied or very satisfied with the program.
* The program increased the students' positive attitude toward school, which we find more important than test scores.
* Ninety percent of the students (55) made a gain in reading.
* Of the 40 students in our program, 28 of them increased by one or more levels on the state assessment of grade-level reading. Our target was 25 students.

Which one best responds to your donor's request?

* The first shows enjoyment. This is often necessary but seldom sufficient to reflect gain.

- The second states satisfaction. Satisfaction, however, is a weak predictor of achievement. Counting high satisfaction could be useful, but it is not distinct in this response.
- The third response is result substitution. We did not raise reading levels but found that other gains are more important.
- The fourth tells how many participants improved but not by how much. If a child went from an assessment score of 48.2 to 48.6, it would be too small of an improvement to mean much.
- The last response gets the ribbon.. It tells the donor (not to mention staff, board, and participants) the difference made . It also says what the yardstick is and states achievement relative to the target set.

Evaluation or Verification?

Many funders ask for your evaluation plan. Most nonprofits say they will do a survey. Neither the request nor the response has much to do with knowing the difference your program made.

A formal evaluation seeks to prove that a program caused a gain for its participants. Such evaluation requires a control group, a double-blind study, and other features that often make the assessment more expensive than the program. For most programs, this level of external scrutiny is not only not warranted, but not helpful. One reason is that "statistical significance" used to show that a result is not random may not amount to practical significance. It can rest on one or two participants in a school class or other setting getting a result. A second factor is that costs are not included. Some programs show gains at a cost that makes them impossible to replicate. A third factor is time. Formal evaluations are completed long after they can be helpful in the current or next round of most programs.

Formal evaluations are assuredly of high importance with major programs fueled by millions of dollars. A Head Start national study, for example, raised significant questions on how long gains last in Head Start. Another evaluation was done of the DARE program, which brings police into schools and takes other steps to reduce drug use among youth. The program was, for a decade, very popular and highly rated by participants. The only problem was that it did very little to reduce drug use. Good to know!

I do want to note my appreciation for some evaluators who put their practice and results together. My favorite example is Michael Quinn Patton, whose early editions of "Utilization-Focused Evaluation" looked at asking and answering questions that programs could directly use to improve performance. He saw—and presumably still sees—little daylight between evaluative thinking and results-oriented thinking.[6]

In results mode, the alternative to evaluation is verification. If you have targets, your question is not what happened, but whether or not you hit the target. The standard shifts from proving that your program caused the gain to showing that the gain would not reasonably have happened without the program. Most donors do not need to know if you are 90% of the reason something good happened or 30%. They want to know if you were necessary for the gain to happen. The rest of this chapter speaks to the discipline needed to demonstrate that.

This is not an evaluation or verification manual. I focus on the distinctions and approaches that bring results into the picture and how to set targets, track to success, and verify. Going back and forth with these core actions, to get them in sync in advance of the action, is critical.

Sources for Confirming Success

Verification begins with some simple distinctions:

1. Factual Records: If 10 persons gained and kept a job, you could look at paystubs or other clear records to confirm that information. Grade-level reading data, clinical health metrics, tons of nutrients monitored in polluted waters could all fall in this category.

    One way to look at facts lies in the distinction between what is objective or subjective. Objective data are based on what reasonable people know to be true given clear evidence. Sure, a few will disagree that the world is round, but this is generally seen to be a fact. The domain of objective data is surprisingly narrow and is not found by looking for numbers. If you find that an average of 76.45 persons said they gained from a program, the precise count is of opinions, not facts. On the other hand, if I count the number of people who have a paystub, few would disagree that this is solid evidence that they have income.

    Once you have facts, you are left with the problem of determining what they mean. If you are considering hiring a person who has been in prison, for example, does that mean they are still a criminal or that they overcame a troubled past? If you look in a person's garbage and see five empty whiskey bottles, does that mean they drink a lot, or that they recently had a big party?

    One possible roadblock to finding facts is that it is not always possible to find facts about participants given confidentiality and privacy laws and concerns. You have two options that can help: first, the patient, client, or participant can choose to give you this information, or, second, you can get verification at a group level. If you ask a guidance counselor for Susie's reading score, it is private. If you give the counselor a list of 20 names and ask how many are now reading at their grade level, most privacy concerns are met. For the purpose of verifying achievement, you do not need to know the names of individuals.

2. Observations: Most results are seen and heard by someone. I like putting observation into program design. Program staff and participants can ask someone to verify whether a given target is being met. I use this for self-improvement. If I am looking to see if my meetings become more effective when I behave differently, I ask someone in the meeting to observe me. Did you notice anything different in what I was doing and, if so, did it make a difference? I do not tell them what I intend. I want to know if they can see it.

    While friends and colleagues are close to the action, they also need the gumption to speak up. How much can a person learn from hearing that they are perfect? How many of us have bosses who have asked for honest feedback then became agitated when we gave it. We cover this later in this chapter. A source that does not require delicacy can be third parties who have a vested interest. A creditor is interested in whether or not a person pays their bills, not on knowing about their participation in a financial management program.

    Another form of observation that is underused is case notes. They are often required of those directly interacting with participants but are seldom used, especially for summing up changes at the end of the program. When I look at case notes from social workers or others, I see similarities in descriptions of what the social worker or other helper did during the program but not much about what was observed as gains. I also see great variety in the level of insight as to what is really going on with the participant.

A weakness in observation of any kind is that different persons may draw different conclusions. Witnesses of crimes or accidents, for example, can be all over the map on what a suspect or situation looked like. Reviewers of proposals give very different ratings for the same proposal. It seems unfair that you could lose a grant because a reviewer gave you 20 points on your need statement while another would have given you 30. The way out of that mess is high inter-rater reliability. This means that raters looking at the same person or act draw about the same conclusions. The best way to get to observer alignment is the use of rubrics. For each category, an observer is to rate on a high to low continuum, with a clear description of each number or level offered. When creating a rubric, I like to start by listening to both those delivering and getting the service. They can be remarkably clear about what progress means in terms of what you can see and hear.[7]

Some rating or ranking frameworks deal with variation by tossing out the highest and lowest ratings on each observation. While this gets you closer to a central tendency, it ignores the insights that often come from observers seeing things that others missed. The extremes can hold great richness.

A different discipline of observation comes from anthropology. I am very impressed with what anthropologists gain from their mode of third-party personal observation. In this ethnographic approach, the standard is often for the observers to be as close to hidden as possible, such that they do not influence what is happening. In other cases, the value lies in becoming visible and asking participants to say what they are doing while they are doing it. The best observations are capturing what is seen and heard long before anyone makes a judgment about what that means. I have found many graduate students with the training to do this very well.

3. Participant comments: We can ask participants to tell us many things: how they liked a program, what they got out of it, whether they were glad they participated, or what they did with what they learned. By far, the most frequent approach is the survey. It is cheap and carries the aroma of precision. Over 90% of the nonprofits I know use surveys as their primary, and often only, tool for assessment. This approach is common, but also problematic.

In some cases, self-reported information may be of the highest value when not intentional to a program. An example is social media and the ways employers look at what is posted as a guide to what a person thinks and believes. This is often made easier by the ways strong or even extreme viewpoints are encouraged on social media platforms. The statements are often more candid and less filtered.

At the same time, self-reports can be very unreliable, especially when the thoughts and actions are seen as undesirable. My physician friends say that when someone reports they have a few drinks per week, they are highly likely to have one to two drinks per day. Anything with a social stigma is likely to be underreported. Anything of high value may well be overreported.

Some dispositions and conditions seem easier for people to see in themselves than in others. If you ask a person if their self-esteem is higher or lower, they may not know. If you ask them if they are happier or have more energy, they may well have an answer. I also find it helps to get to images. Rather than defining energy in any complicated way, ask if they feel they have more gas in the tank or more or less bounce in their step.

When participants self-report, it is critical to know if they are speaking about themselves or the group. When someone says that everyone in the program showed great enthusiasm, they are not reporting on themselves. I like the guideline of asking participants clearly to either speak for themselves or for the group. If the latter, a caution is merging personal views with observation. "No one liked that module," may mean that the respondent and one other person did not like it.

Surveys, Surveys, Surveys

Surveys are almost synonymous with evaluation for many non-profits. Most programs rely on them as their primary source of information on achievement and broader impact. This section is not meant to be a primer on constructing surveys, but rather ways to approach using surveys to avoid their striking shortcomings when it comes to clearly depicting results.

Here are major survey challenges, followed by suggestions:

1. **They focus on what people think rather than how they behave:** Are you satisfied? Do you feel more empowered? Was the program of value? Most of us respond with an opinion or impression.

   Rather than asking if people are exercising more, ask them how many times they exercised last week. Rather than asking them to rate the program on a scale of 1 to 10, ask them to list their top three takeaways and what they have done with them.

2. **Multiple choice questions define the options:** These are your choices—pick one. Adding a category of "Other" at the end of the alternatives is of little help. The frame has been set, and the opportunity to listen carefully to the words the participant chose to use is lost.

   Most surveys stay away from open-ended questions even though this is often where the insights really come. These are not as time consuming to code into categories as you might think.

3. **Numerical scales have unknown distances between numbers:** On a 10-point scale, one person's six is another's four or eight. While a midpoint anchor helps, the numbers are rarely precise in the mind of the respondent. When I ask for a rank ordering, some items may be very close together, and some far apart on a ranking. We have no way of knowing.

   Having clarity on the midpoint can help. Even better is a forced end point where you ask respondents to check one extreme or the other and put everything else in the middle. This has higher inter-rater reliability, especially when people rate themselves.

4. **A positive tilt can sneak in:** When a survey question asks how much value a person received from a program, the presumption is that the program had some value. It may have had none. At the least, qualify the question with that: What value, if any, did the program…? Another example: midpoints on survey responses that nudge toward success. I recently took a survey offered by a large regional health system in which one question asked of my overall experience. The options were:

Excellent   Very Good   Good   Fair   Unsatisfactory

Not only was the midpoint good, rather than so-so, but the end points were skewed. The opposite of excellent is bad or really poor, not unsatisfactory.

5. **Response rate is often very low:** Often no more than 10 to 20% of those given a survey complete it. The problem, then, is whether they are an accurate reflection on all persons in the program. Almost assuredly, they are not. In my experience, those very negative or positive are much more likely to complete than those without strong views. Also, available time (which can correlate with income and time opportunity) may influence response rate.

A simple step is follow-up reminders, which does raise response rates. Another approach is to see how close the sample mirrors the full population of participants in any demographic factor that might reasonably create variation in responses. Income, gender identity,sex, ethnicity, age, and education levels often show patterns.

6. **Anonymity makes assessment impersonal:** It is an article of faith that people are more honest when their name

is not added to survey responses. This creates two big problems. First, there is no way to follow up on responses you want to learn more about. Second, the personal program ends on an impersonal note. Results are best when owned and shared, not masked for individuals who experience them.

Ask participants whether you might be able to follow up if you want to learn more and, if the response is yes, ask for an email or phone number. I have found that well above 80% of participants say fine and give their information. This comes at the end of the survey and has minimal influence on what respondents say.

7. **Comparative achievement is not possible:** When nonprofits create their own questions, they lose the ability to compare responses with many other groups. That only comes with standard, well-tested questions asked in hundreds of surveys. This is vital information for any group seeking great improvement.[8]

I work with clients who use assessments such as the CDC Healthy Days assessment and USDA Hunger scale. Comparability to aggregate groups and populations based on demographics and other factors are built in. A caution: many such metrics are meant to assess populations and changes within large numbers. Attribution is tricky when employed to see the effects of a program. A senior's take on their number of healthy days may have more to do with an argument that morning with their grandson than a nonprofit program later that day.

8. **They are snapshots:** Surveys are like pictures—they speak to what is currently present rather than what has gone before or might come after.

Multiple check-ins are critical to see patterns of volatility and stability in almost any viewpoint. Also, surveys are seen as located at the end of the program, which misses their value as a check-in during a program to see what is happening.

Many of these drawbacks are overcome with help from survey experts. They can readily spot common mistakes. One example: lumping two or more topics in one question. If you ask, "To what extent was the program informative and engaging?" you have no idea which part of the question is addressed in the answer.

Surveys can assuredly be of value. Many of them come from viewing this tool not as the ending point, but as a starting one. Results 1st works with groups, for example, to use surveys to identify individuals with whom there is a need to go deeper or aspects of the program that are not yet working for them.

Expectations and Satisfaction

Two of the most common measures used to reflect nonprofit accomplishment have a surprisingly weak connection to participant achievement. The first is the extent to which a program met expectations. The second is the level of satisfaction with the program. Let's look at each.

The first problem with expectations is that we do not know what they are. One person might expect a nice lunch and the chance to reconnect with colleagues. One might look forward to learning something new. Still another might be looking for validation of what they are now doing. There is also a possibility that the participant did not arrive with any expectations. The last thing we want to do is give credit to a program for meeting low or manufactured expectations.

One of the many values in setting targets with participants is that targets can become expectations. Henry Ford has a wonderful observation on this: "Whether you think you can or you can't, you're right." Studies in education have found that when a teacher is told that an incoming student has great potential, that student does better academically than if no such message is given. If the expectation is that a participant will achieve a specific result, the chances rise that they will do so.[9]

Expectations, however, lose value when they are based on what a person does rather than what they achieved. In performance reviews, rating categories often include "met expectations," "exceeded expectations," and "fell below expectations." Expectations often vary in ways that are unfair to some employees. They can also readily reward behavior unrelated or even counterproductive to high achievement. The employee came to all meetings on time. They responded to requests. They supervised other employees. They never raised divergent thoughts and were team players. In short, they did the expected things.

Now, to satisfaction, where one challenge is the same as with expectations: we do not know what factors cause it. One parent or caregiver may be satisfied because a program keeps their child safe with an after-school program. Another may not be satisfied until the child does better academically. A patron is unsatisfied that the bartender will not pour them another one, and the establishment is pleased they will not drive home drunk. And in meetings, I find that the chair who speaks a lot is much more satisfied than the attendees who have to listen to them.

A second problem is that satisfaction is a low bar. Businesses define a satisfied customer as one with no reason to complain. Much more consequential are the number of persons who are either highly satisfied or greatly dissatisfied. Business has long known that a highly satisfied customer is far more likely to buy again and tell their friends about their product than a satisfied one. I see similar patterns with nonprofit participants. The highly satisfied participant is the one who gained a lot from the program and told their friends about it. When a program says that 90% of participants are satisfied or highly satisfied, it masks the huge difference between these categories. The greatly dissatisfied customer is often the best source of information relevant to improving a program. They are also a solid opportunity. Unlike satisfied customers, where you have to galvanize interest, you already have their attention. You just need to pivot from a negative to a positive experience.

While satisfaction is generally put on a continuum (eg, how satisfied were you on a scale of 1 to 10), many companies only count the 1's and the 10's. I like going further to get at the extremes—raving fans and those profoundly disillusioned. They are literally off the charts. A client in Seattle portrayed this on the survey by showing space between the continuum and the end points.

People in the middle are actually the toughest to move on a scale. People who are satisfied are complacent. They have no reason to think about you further. With high dissatisfaction or raving fans, you already have their attention. It is easier to see a major change when a group solves a problem or engages a fan to help promote their services.

With high satisfaction, I generally see two factors present that apply to nonprofit programs as readily as to those getting an oil change or buying a car.

The first is a personal touch. The salesman or tech support folks really understood me and my needs. The bank teller remembered my name. My mentor was incredibly engaging. Nonprofits who focus on the programs and believe that all of their staff are great miss the reality that some do the personal touch far better than others. A way to see this, if your program is large enough, is to see if raving fans distribute about equally over all sites and persons who deliver the program. In most cases, they will not.

The second factor creating high satisfaction is the unexpected. When we get the expected service at any level, we may initially be surprised but will soon see it as routine. This leads to a satisfied customer and shows the relationship between expectation and satisfaction levels. The routine is rarely awesome. When I interviewed the highly satisfied customers of Trustco Bank branches and Transworld Entertainment store customers, I kept hearing stories of going the extra mile—the store associate who delivered the desperately needed CD player to the home of the beleaguered dad who did not have to pick it up for his daughter's birthday. In the nonprofit realm, I interviewed a person in a program to get and keep a job in Seattle. The participant was amazed to see their counselor parked nearby to make sure they got out the door on time for the first few days of work. More surprises seem to come from persons rather than from systems. These same considerations apply to nonprofit programs, both large and small.

This also applies to strong dissatisfaction. The passenger did not expect to sit for five hours on the tarmac on a hot plane. The participant in a workshop did not expect the presenter to be unclear and disorganized. The personal touch can just as easily go south as north.

One way this can happen is a disconnect between experience and result. My friend Susie Bowie speaks of going to a watch repair shop. She gets full support of an empathetic store associate. She learns that the repairs come with the highest quality standards. Her response: I just want my watch to work. Customer experience is no more of value than customer satisfaction if the person does not get their need met.

Before you can ask people to explain their high satisfaction or dissatisfaction, you have to know who they are. One way is to flag those off the continuum in either direction on a survey. Another starts with word analysis on open-ended survey questions or a reflection format. You or a word software program look for how frequently words that mean "good" and those that mean "great" are used. A person who finds a program very helpful and very good is satisfied. A person who says "ecstatic" or "changed my life" is highly satisfied. This is not an easy sort, especially given how many people lean toward superlatives in everyday speech. If many things are awesome or amazing, nothing can stand out.

Built-In Assessment

In great programs, participants as well as staff get and use data to track and verify achievement as the program unfolds. Evaluation moves from outside to inside the program as an integral part of what happens. Here are two approaches I find very useful:

1. Share the target and ask participants to tell you when they hit it: In far too many cases, the meanings and data of assessments during a program are known only to program staff. The participant is the subject but not the force for change. Here is an example of how this can be structured for workshops and other educational programs:

   a. Get participant agreement on the result as the program begins: My target is that 25 of the 35 of you present will tell us at the end of the program something they want to do differently as a result of what they gain today. My target is that 15 of you will, within two weeks, name some specific steps you have taken to apply that. Does that seem like a reasonable target?

b. Check in during the program to see if participants are on track to achieve the target: We have completed four of the eight sessions. How many of you have picked up on something you want to remember and use in order to improve what participants get from your own programs? Let's get some examples of what you want to change.

c. At the end, ask what will stick with participants and what they will do with it. Experience suggests that when participants in a program, before they leave, take time to think about what they want to remember and how they will use it, chances that they will actually do so will soar. Could I get a few examples please? Show of hands to see how many of you intend to do something differently within the next two weeks?

d. Follow-up in two to three weeks: Can you name anything you have done differently as a result of this program? If so, what, if any, gain did it bring?

In this example, there is simply no daylight between program and verification. They are together. Our program has two parts: action and reflection. After each week (or day) of project work, we pause as part of this program to give you time to think about, record, and share your thoughts, feelings, and changes. Reflections can also be combined with diaries and other open-ended formats, which we will discuss in a later section of this chapter.

2. Whenever possible, embed assessments that track use of information. Many programs focus assessment on

before and after knowledge. This is more predictive of short-term memory than of change in behavior. The more promising capability assessments focus on skills. Can the person apply what they learned? Certificates from Google and many other companies can literally certify the ability to create or fix something. I once worked with the CEO of Transworld Entertainment, which owned over one thousand stores on what he called "The Great Store Manager Program." To get that designation, after an intense training program, the store manager was given a set of simulations to which they had to respond immediately. For example: here is a list of your sales last week, organized by music genres and end caps versus aisle displays. Given this data, how will you set up the display space next week? Simulations also reflect attributes such as handling stress— the same stress store managers and nonprofit leaders face daily in their organizations.

Many programs embed benchmark assessments to show progress. Be careful to ensure that they predict success. This is important whether the assessments are your own or come from a national or product level. I recall looking at two curricula widely used by preschool networks: Creative Curriculum and High Scopes. Two of my clients looked to see whether one was better at tracking kids' progress in getting school-ready. At that time, one curriculum was chosen by many preschools because it was much easier for teachers to understand and embrace. The benchmark assessments in the other, however, proved much more accurate forecasts of school readiness.

Qualitative and Quantitative

Traditionally, nonprofits and their funders see these terms as separated. On the one hand, you have numbers, and on the other, you have the richness of experience. Program staff see numbers as missing richness. Those who deal in numbers call findings focussed on experience as soft and squishy. Participant stories can be seen as either the soul of a program or anecdotes with no context depending on where one sits.

When I asked a group in workforce development how many jobs they created, they pushed back saying they created quality jobs. So, I asked what that meant to them. They told me that quality meant that the job:

* Paid a living wage
* Had health benefits
* Offered mobility after six months

Fine. Let's count the jobs that have a livable wage, health benefits, and some mobility. With qualities, you define what enrichment and gain mean. You get to numbers by counting the persons who get to that enrichment.

One term to use carefully is "measurable." While it is typically seen as going to quantities (as in, "What are your measurable objectives?"), you can also measure degrees of quality once you define them. The starting point is not counting, but deciding what counts. In my view, if you can carefully describe a quality, you can find a way to see how much of it is present.[10]

Interviews and Conversations

When it comes to understanding achievement, nothing beats listening to people who get it. The richest veins are those persons who are highly satisfied and those who are really unhappy. You can then change programs to get more of the former, less of the latter.

One reason personal and group interviews are so rare is a presumption of high cost. *We just can't afford the time to speak individually with participants. We have to use surveys.* Think again. Assume that conversations take five minutes to set up, 10 minutes to have, and 10 minutes to capture—a person can do two per hour. If I pay interviewers $50 per hour, that's $25 per interview. Take a program with 50 participants: 30 persons may be deemed highly satisfied and five may be presumed to be very unsatisfied. Those 35 persons will cost $875. Surveys have systems for getting responses, entering data, and making sense of what was said. Interviews and conversations do that even more while keeping the discipline behind the curtain.

Here are suggestions to make these deeper dives result-based:

1. We're just talking: I find that I get more from the participant when they see this as an informal exchange rather than formal interview. You can bring a lot of discipline in without it ever appearing. Yes, you sacrifice the rigor of comparability. Where that is needed, use a formal interview schedule and do not vary from it. In most cases, however, you are only interested in insight. The deeper you go, the more individualized this may become. With informal formats, it is even more important to define confidentiality. I like two statements: 1) You will have a chance to review and change what I write up from this discussion, and 2) Your name will not be attached to anything you say without your permission. And one guideline: avoid saying that what they tell you is confidential. Rather, it is their name connected to the comments that you do not share without agreement.

2. No need to please me: Do not ask the person delivering the service to conduct the interviews. How could a participant not be super positive when speaking to the per-

son who helped them so much. I find it acceptable for board members to conduct the interviews in that they are seen as playing an oversight, rather than a delivery role. It also helps to make clear that the interviewer does not know much about the organization. One might say, "I purposefully did not read a lot about the program or the group offering it. I want to get your take on this, not look to confirm my impressions."

3. Ask for examples: The best form of probing is not to ask why people say something. They may not know. Ask, rather, for examples or illustrations of the general points and conclusions they offer. I learned this the hard way when we hired people to interview subscribers to a journal I had started called "Innovating." We would ask people how they liked the last issue. "Wonderful," some said. We then asked, "What was an article that you really liked?" We then heard, "Oh, it was all so great. I don't think I could mention one article in particular." We noted high satisfaction, but not high value.

4. Dig for the nuggets: Capture examples as well as key words and expressions that seem unusual or insightful. I worked with a seniors volunteer group who were being prepared to call participants in a program. They spoke of getting to the "nuggets," so we developed a guide for interviewers on how to mine for them. Just as miners could sift sand and see the nuggets, these seniors wanted to do the same with comments that shined.[11]

With about 30 participants, you can talk to everyone. With more, you need a sampling technique. In addition to making sure those selected reflect the full participant group on such factors such as ethnicity, race, age, sex, and gender identity, I like reflecting where they are on levels of satisfaction. If a survey tells me that 20 of 100 are highly satisfied and five are very dissatisfied, I can start to see patterns.

When do you speak individually or with groups? I find it depends on the purpose. If I want to get as deep as possible with what is going on with individuals, I like one-on-one formats. If I want to see participants build on what others say and observe where views depart and converge, I like small groups—seldom more than six to eight persons. The group approach may inhibit divergent viewpoints, but it can also gain visibility for key points. For example, a city agency in Seattle that ran a naturalist program for school classes in its parks was losing participants. I spoke with 10 teachers to learn why this was happening. They spoke to the cost of transportation and of time away from learning tested material. Once we covered that, I asked why they chose to come. The first to speak said that another teacher had recommended it. This led to a chorus of comments on how the teachers ignored the many brochures they saw for enrichment experiences. They had to hear it from teachers whom they respected. This view was overwhelming. The program stopped printing brochures and putting smiley faces in social media. Numbers built the response to a level that compelled action.

Reflections and Diaries

No matter how informal, discussion directs content at least to some extent. In contrast, when people are thinking or speaking to themselves, we have some assurance that what they say is not filtered by what we think others want to hear. I like two formats that yield not only great insight as to how a person interacts with a program, but also learning and meaning for the writer.

The first approach is reflections built into the program: This summer community project has two parts. You will work to build three community gardens. You will pause once a week to reflect on what you are thinking, feeling, and doing. Here's an example from a Reflections Log used to understand the impacts participating in an intensive mock trial experience had on high school students in Washington State. The Jefferson Community Center's team finished 18th in Washington State. What makes this remarkable is that this was the only mock trial team in Seattle that was open to all willing participants. With all other teams, only the highest-achieving students were invited.

Here are a few passages which each reflected more than half of the respondents in two areas of focus:

Any growth you have seen in yourself:

"I became much more conscientious in being receptive to ideas."

"I am finding more and more logical ways to answer questions. My posture has changed, and impressing people with speech and presentation is no longer nerve-wrecking."

"I am more open to ideas. I am more open about my own ideas, too. I can now express them without struggling."

Value the mock trial had for you:

"This experience is one I see of more importance than anything else that I've participated in. We all see each other as family, and so we're open to admitting mistakes. I feel comfortable around them and know I can openly ask for help when I need it. This is not the case at school, as I feel surrounded by judgmental people."

"I place the mock trial as one of the major influences in my life, right next to competitive varsity sports, because of the dedication and commitment required and the benefits I gain in public speaking, knowledge of court proceedings, and analytical skills."

"I do value my education and getting good grades, but the mock trial is almost of equal value. I say this because I do value my team and how we functioned. This was also my first time doing anything really competitive, and I did want us to succeed."

A colleague and I read all of the logs submitted and did not have a problem seeing major patterns. One was that close to half the reflections were about a skill students learned, and the other half were about the confidence to use knowledge. Another common thread was the power of group interactions that had a result focus. These participants did not report on playing nicely together. They said they worked together to win their mock trial.

The second format, which has little or no structure, is the diary. Just write what comes to mind and heart. I like the digital formats that simulate page turnings in a hard copy diary. A number of older participants like to hand write. Diaries are personal, yet I have found that many people are happy to share them with a trusted program staff member. In this case, you are looking for intimacy rather than distance from those delivering the program.

Still another approach works well with large numbers. You can use a Learning Log format that prompts presenters to pause for entries with a slide like this:

Let's pause for a minute to give you time to make an entry in your learning log. You have a format to note questions, likely take-aways, and names of persons you have identified so far for possible follow-up. Anything you want to remember goes here.

I have observed sessions of up to 400 persons and find that, with few exceptions, participants do turn to the log and make some entries rather than hit their phones or the bathroom.

Result Stories

Organizations love to tell stories about how a person in a program has made amazing strides. The graver the plight, the more impressive the transformation. Stories are told by words and pictures on websites, in proposals, project and annual reports, and at conferences. Stories can be compelling. Few of us keep in mind the statistics of a program. Most of us, however, remember a few great stories about how lives were changed. Yet many funders and onlookers dismiss stories as soft or anecdotal. They are planted on one side of the qualitative/quantitative divide. You can bring stories across to be seen as real data by taking three steps:

1. **Ensure that the person tells his or her own story.** While the words of the PR writer or the authoritative narrator on the video may bring a tear to the eye, the best stories are autobiographical. The storyteller need not be glib or polished. They simply need to be authentic. If the person is not good at writing or even fully literate, no problem. Ask them to say it, and you write and read it back. Is this what you want to say?

   Most nonprofits ignore this first element when they present at conferences. Nonprofit staff speak for the program and the participants. I saw this problem early in my career while doing self-help projects in low-income Cherokee, Black, and White Appalachian communities. We put in place a rule that no staff person should speak for residents. They had to be present. Several distinguished conference planners took us off their agenda. They said it did not fit their format of experts and professionals speaking. We were fine with being excluded on those grounds.

   Stories are different from testimonials. "A great

read… a real page turner." "This program was amazing—I loved it." "Robyn Meyer was just great." This kind of praise is, at best, abstract. It tells you little, and I suggest you avoid it and get to longer statements that tell a full story. Most are told within a page. None are told within a sentence.

2. **Make sure that the story says just how the program helped create the gain.** People get better for lots of reasons. I recall a verification call with a student in Connecticut who was listed as a success in an after-school program. The nonprofit had taken credit, assuming that, because the student participated in the program and achieved much better grades, the first had caused the second. The conversation went as follows: "Hello. I'm calling because we are interested in how kids are doing in middle school these days. So, let's start there. How are you doing in school this year?"

"Great—a lot better. I was getting C's, and now I am getting B's and sometimes an A."

"Wow, how did that happen?"

The student replied that his grandfather moved in with him. He told his grandson that each marking period he would give him $25 for every B and $50 for every A. The school did not solely cause the gain. Thankfully for the nonprofit, this example does not end here. The person making the call followed up by noting that the money motivated the student, but wondered if he needed any support once the money got his attention.

"Yes, I got help. I was in this after-school program, and they really helped me to learn what I needed to know to get some B's."

In this same call, the student commented that what mattered to him was the connection with a student aide who used to be like him in high school—doing poorly and tuning out. He said that person was by the far the biggest help. The program had assumed that the key was the certified teachers whom the aides supported. Once a number of students had comments similar to the first student, they changed the ratio of teachers and aides and saved money while increasing results.

Another example also illustrates the influence of individuals. One woman told the story seeker that an arts program had made a huge difference in her life. When asked what part of the program was so impactful, here is what she put in her Result Story:

What was it about the program that influenced me? Actually, it was a person. J was the heart of the program. She exudes the virtues that she preaches. She spills over with love, is always joyful, and has contagious positive feelings.

The management sage, Peter Drucker, once observed that a program and its success factors are never described in the same way by participants as they are by program designers and deliverers.

3. **Locate the stories such that they turn anecdotes into data.** If you offer a story, the reader or viewer has no idea how many stories you have. You have to tell them. For example: "Of the 80 persons in the program, we have 20 stories at this same level of gain. Would you like to see the others?" This is the toughest step, so let's pause to look at ways to do it.

The best approach is to generate a list before you

start contacting participants. Put all participants into one of three groups:

a. Those fully successful. These are the participants who hit or exceeded the target.

b. Those partially successful. They did not hit the target but made some clear gains.

c. Those not successful. They had little or no known gain. Include those who dropped out.

If you put all or most people in the high-success category, take another look. You want evidence. You can then start by getting stories from those in each category who are known to the program. Then, you want to purposefully pick a person in each that you do not know as well. You want to make sure the distribution covers everyone, not just the persons with whom the program has had the most contact. A different approach is to start with random selection, then profile the group based on level of success and demographic, or other factors.

With lists of people in hand, sure—start by generating stories of those highly successful. Then go to a few people who were not successful. Investors love this because they know that you are unlikely to make changes if they are all storybook endings. The nonprofit gains the most in knowing what to do to help others—whether that means program refinement or getting them into a different program that is more likely to forecast success for them. You want to get all stories completed before you start making sense of them. Then, you want to pull in stories that make different points, especially about which elements in the program led to achievement.

Email **info@results1st.com** for examples of great stories and how to use them.

When Do You Take Credit?

At the beginning of this chapter, I noted that investors most often want to know if the gain would have happened if your program did not exist. Can you attribute the gain to the program, or might other things going on better explain the change? You do not need to be the top factor. You just have to be seen as necessary.

The result story format described above is a good start. When you ask participants why something has happened and give them free reign to respond, they will either put you in the picture or not. My rule of thumb is that you want to be among the first three factors a person mentions as helping them achieve at your target level. At times, participants can also tell you how many others were likely to have found the program a key to success. From one story:

> Jai cannot save everyone. I think she had the success she did with me with just over half of the participants. You have to have some spark or desire on which she can build. She does not change who she is. Participants have to change who they are.

What an insight. You will come across jewels like this one when you give people permission to speak in their own words.

This personal approach is critical but has its limits. Many of us do not always know why we did something. A different approach brings in the "absence of program" baseline. Here are four ways to help establish that.

1. Trend lines: For any program, look at results for the last three years and extend the line through the next year. This is what is most likely to happen. If results are much

better than that, and there is no other big factor that is different, this contributes to a reasonable conclusion that your program made the difference.

2. Nothing else big happened. Trend lines can be interrupted by a major change such as a new principal in a school, a fire or flood in the neighborhood, or major change in funding of mainstream programs. If you cannot see, and participants do not name, another big major shift, this adds confidence that the trend would continue.

3. Expert opinion. You can turn to those who most understand the population you serve. Guidance counselors are an example—give them the names of the persons in your program and ask them how many of those on the list are likely to achieve the result intended (whether it be higher grades, lower suspensions, avoiding juvenile court or pregnancy, or something else) in the next year if they did not participate in your program. You are just looking for a total number, not information on any given student. In most cases, aggregate information does not violate privacy and confidentiality requirements.

4. Comparison groups. If you have a clearly defined group of participants, you may be able to select a similar group which is not in the program to see differences. This is not a formal control group, and you are not claiming statistical precision. It is a reasonable comparison group and can be drawn for either another group or a set of individuals with the same demographic and other characteristics. Here's an example: I worked with a group of investors using the "I Have a Dream" model. This is the approach of a person or foundation saying to a class as early as first grade that if a student graduates high school

and gets into a college, that the philanthropy will pay all their costs of college.

They selected an elementary school that had five first-grade classes, one of which was very similar in demographic and other factors to the classroom selected for the program. After high school, and considering only the students in both groups who had remained at the school from the first grade on, six more students (35%) graduated and entered college in the Dream Announcement class than the comparison group. The larger the difference, the less likely it would occur by chance.

TRY IT

1. Insert a new question in your next feedback form asking if the respondent would agree to speak with you if you wanted to learn more. See how many say yes then call or email two persons who reported high gains two weeks after the program. Go deeper into what in the program most prompted success as well as added impacts.

2. Ask and guide a board member or donor to follow up with another participant reporting high gains. Use the guidelines for a result story defined in the chapter. See what you learned that can improve your program. Also, see if this has any effect on the level of engagement of the person doing this.

CHAPTER 4

Learn and Change

A foundation is deciding which of two groups to choose for a large grant meant to help house the homeless. One established and well-regarded nonprofit is at a comparatively high level of achievement, which they sustain each year. The second group is relatively new and achieves a lower number of persons housed for the same money. In each of its three years of existence, however, it has increased its homeless housing by 50%. Which is the better group for a grant? The second one is highly likely to surpass the established group. Improvement curve is far more predictive of high achievement than either years of existence or consistency of programs.

Traditionally, a chapter with this focus would be called "Learning." Many terms, however, take on a different meaning when you put results first. Learning in my context means change—not stocking up information for future use. No one can say how much they have learned and how little they have changed.[12]

Calling All Mistakes

It is tough to learn from the mistakes you never made. Sadly, most organizations scurry away from shortfalls or look to blame them on outside sources. Psychologists call this an external locus of control. When things do not work out well, it is the fault of some outside force. Bureaucracy, the weather, the bad economy. I have heard principals say that the reason test scores dipped this year was that they had a slow class. The opposite tendency is to put responsibility on yourselves. We did not figure out how to overcome that obstacle. It's our fault. That's an internal locus of control. Here's the difference:

> George X. Cuse: I am sad to report that we lost $10,000 at the bazaar. I'll pass out the financial income and expenses, but the big point is that it rained. We had such great plans, and the weather forecast had a 95% chance of sunshine just one day before the event. Things like this do happen, of course. Better luck to us next year.

> Jeff Ownit: I really don't want to stand here because I am responsible for much of the $10,000 loss we experienced at the bazaar. Sure, it rained. But there was always a chance this would happen, and I did not have a contingency plan. I called the vendor that made up all of those sandwiches that we had to toss out. I asked him if he could have reduced our bill if I called him late the night before to cancel. He said sure, that the cost would have dropped from $2,600 to $500. He would not have taken perishables out of the freezer and he would not have incurred the labor to make the sandwiches. A busted deal reduction was possible with other vendors as well.

> Who do you want to run the bazaar next year?

The Director of Citicorp Venture Capital told me of a time when he and colleagues were grilling an entrepreneur who was seeking an investment. The fellow admitted that he had failed at two previous start ups. Peter asked him one more question: "When do you need our money?" The entrepreneur asked the investors why they were going to invest in him after his previous bad decisions. They replied that he did not think he had any mistakes left to make. The first problem with people who have not made mistakes is that you don't know what they will do when this happens. The second problem is their lack of honesty.

To travel the patch of internal control you need not go public. The conversation may just be with yourself. Marshall Goldsmith, in his insightful book "Triggers," describes how he uses a self-improvement approach that checks in at the end of the day with a series of, "Did I do my best to…" This is refined self-improvement. If change does not happen at a personal level, it will not happen at an organizational level.

Asking Questions

I was once asked by the CEO of KeyCorp, a large banking group, to help the company compete for a big quality award by showing how much of a learning organization they were. I decided to attend a cross section of meetings with a pad that had a line down the middle. One column was "questions," the other, "statements." When I went back to the leader, I observed that if they were a learning organization, they had an interesting way of reflecting that. I tallied over 100 assertions for every question asked.

Questions are the lifeblood of learning. In fact, if I had to name one factor that forecasts degree of improvement, it is degree of inquisitiveness. This is a focused inquiry. Here are some characteristics of great questions:

They encourage thinking before speaking. Educators have long worked with teachers and students on the difference between fat and skinny questions. Skinny questions can be answered with a yes or a no or with a stock response. How are you today? Fine. How was your flight? Good. Many such questions are born in ritual where the exchange seems almost obligatory. If you can predict the answer, why ask the question?

They enable musing. A great question sendoff is, "What if...?" It takes us out of current realities to look at different possibilities. My friend and mentor, Isaac Asimov, believed this question was the starting point for all science fiction. What if robots were as smart as people? What if you could not tell the difference between a robot and a human being? His questions are as relevant to AI as they were to robotics. If the question assumes current reality, so too will the responses.

They lead to other questions. When I hear questions asked in an organization, I watch for what happens. Here is what I see: In about half the cases, no one pauses to answer the question. Opinions keep flying. In about 25%, someone does attempt to answer the question, then the discussion continues after this brief interruption. The last 25% of the instances bring more questions that build a spirit of inquiry. People stop answering and start wondering. When this happens, learning begins.

They are short. How many times have we all heard an audience member start asking their question by first giving their opinion, experience, or context. By the time they get to the question, most have tuned out. One host of a morning cable show offers his opinions first—sometimes long-winded. Guests who want to return know that they should start with agreement.

Another checklist I like speaks to the characteristics of a strong learning question for organizations:

* You can bring information to bear on the question. It is not philosophical or theoretical.
* More than one answer is possible, and the askers have not already made up their minds as to which answer is correct.

- Questioners are very interested in getting responses to use themselves, not solely as surrogates for others.
- The person or group asking the question can say how they will use the answer once they get it.

Do not confuse a good questioner with one who continually says, "I question that." This is a statement, not an inquiry.

Inquiry is a practice, not a mindset, and prompts can really help. One is to hold a "What If" hour every quarter or month to focus on something that most agree could be better. It could be the organization or a program within it. This approach works with groups as large as 15 and as small as two. All present start a question that begins "What If?" The group selects one question to pursue. The bolder the alternative, the better. Stick with it, asking for those present to suspend opinion and even logic until the group has taken the idea as far as possible.

A more general prompt starts with dividing every meeting or other interaction into questions first and opinions second. "We have all read this drafted strategic plan." "Does anyone have a question about it?" "No comments yet, please." In most discussions, I hear assumptions that should have first surfaced as inquiry to clarify and confirm them.

Lessons Learned

"We learned our lesson." Great, and what did you do differently? Most of us learn and relearn lessons many times before we change. We need help in both defining and using lessons. Here's an example of a format I have used to harness the power of a lesson. It comes from a community renewal project TRI mounted with the residents of Stump Creek, PA.

- The Experience: Almost every time we went right to renewal work in the early months of renewal, we struggled to keep up resident energy. It was more meetings, more Saturday workdays. Enthusiasm turned to drudgery. On the other hand, on those occasions when some reminder of community and the way residents help each other came in, we noticed that energy was sustained.

- The Lesson: Reframe most of the steps in terms of shared experience and community symbols. These are more important than the Saturday sign-up sheet.
- The Change: Immediately bring in reminders of community. One example came from the new water line residents installed. When done, they had their names all painted on the water tower. They saw this every time they drove into town.

Note the tone is positive. What will we do differently, rather than what did we do wrong?

Hold quarterly Lessons Learned Forums in your organization. The price of admission is coming with a lesson in a format such as the one above. Even if the staff and volunteer numbers are very small, this is an intentional practice with great returns. Indeed, with just two persons, the relationship may be completely open, but with friendship and camaraderie, that can make explicit learning less likely. The key is to push out the experience quickly and spend most of the time pondering what to do differently. Lessons are a springboard to start something, not a point of closure.

Best Practices

Many publications and gatherings are billed as offering best practices. Come and learn. In most such offerings, the term "best" is not clear. To put results first, we first want to know what has been achieved by the use of a practice. Without this rigor, the practices with the lowest impact may be the most popular and attractive. I have also sat in on convenings where most of the talking is done by groups with low achievement.

Best practices are widely available. Many practices to achieve high results for persons with drug addiction, homelessness, obesity, and other afflictions are offered on websites and publications of national organizations. The discouraging part is that many groups report remarkably low numbers of downloads or feedback on use of their research. According to a World Bank study in 2014, for example, nearly one-third of the reports available as PDF's on their website had never been downloaded even once.[13]

Most nonprofits seem to prefer to get new ideas from others rather than from research and clarity on what works and what elements are critical in any application of a practice. This can lead, in my experience, to a lot of generalizations that are too general to help. How many presentations have I seen with the best practice of, "Involve the residents," or, "Build trust before acting." Here's an example of a practice I applied that was a great power. It focused on guidelines for board member giving. At TRI, I had some board members who could give $100,000 and some for whom $100 was a lot. We had been using the guideline of, "Give what you can," which meant that no one was clear on expectations. The best practice I heard at a conference and was able to apply was to ask prospective board members to commit to making you one of each board member's top four charities. The point shared was that the nonprofit wanted board members who gave it priority.

When, with board approval, I put this guideline into place. One board member resigned. He noted he had many contributions of a larger amount. He did say he appreciated the principle, and he continued to give the same reasonably small annual amount. Three board members added a significant amount to annual giving, noting they needed to up their gifts to us to make us number four on gift size. This little guideline, actionable in short order, almost doubled annual board contributions and made everyone more comfortable now that they knew our expectations.

Practices are different from models, which are fully articulated approaches. I cover models and their role in spreading and moving a needle in Chapter 10. In sharp contrast to best practices, models must carry a great deal of disciplined information as well as an instruction manual. Best practices must be specific, but they need not be doctrine.

Benchmarking

"Name the two groups you consider most comparable to you and say how you are similar to and different from them." I like putting this in applications and find that many nonprofits have weak answers. They either say they are unique or that they know very little about these other groups' work, even if they have partnered in programs. Benchmarking is the systematic study of a group that does something exceptionally well. It is generally most effective when it digs down into specifics. While you get some value from reading what groups write and share through best practices and lessons learned, the real insights from benchmarking come from direct observation. You get it when you see it.

Benchmarking must be highly selective, which can be difficult. Rating and ranking services such as GuideStar and Charity Navigator, for example, contain information on finances and compliances as well as plentiful narratives of values, missions and visions, and beliefs. They are largely silent, however, on effectiveness. Many funders—even locally—may not have that kind of information either. A good starting point is clues from persons who have worked with or been helped by other nonprofits. Another is groups that publish their accomplishments and include such areas as turnover and board development. Most inquiries do not hinge on being in the same geography. A great organization in staff or volunteer retention three states away is of more value than just a good one next door.

It helps to be very specific. Almost all organizations are strong in a few areas and weak in others. You might want to learn how other groups:

* Get high-performing people when they can't pay much
* Retain high-performing persons for at least five years
* Build assessments into program designs
* Use their results to raise more money
* Attract great and diverse board members

There is a high probability that a group exists that does any of the above-listed items very well. Will they help you? In his book, "All You Have to Do Is Ask," Wayne Baker points out that as much as 90% of help that is provided in the workplace occurs only after requests for help have been made. He notes that most of us underestimate the capacity and willingness others have to support us even when the environment is considered competitive.

Benchmarking is a rigorous pursuit. It is not a site visit or a chance to exchange ideas or make new friends. It is a chance to learn how a group achieves what you are not achieving now. Here are three guidelines:

1. Before you go, read. You want to be up on what the organization does so you do not have to waste time learning the basics on site. I have actually seen a benchmarking team quiz each other to make sure they not only knew the organization being benchmarked, but that they had the key numbers in their heads.

2. When you visit, keep the group size small—at both your end and theirs. A group of two to three persons will get

far deeper than a group of 10. Also, leave anyone who can't resist talking too much at home.

3. Observe what they do whenever possible. In particular, get to the shop floor. If the group says they have a great case manager who galvanizes action among participants, see if you can sit in. Listening to leaders opine on what is done is far less useful than seeing staff in action.

Another powerful form of benchmarking takes you down the hall rather than to the airport. If you have three or more persons doing the same job, ask yourself if all of them are equally effective. They seldom are. This is an opportunity for significant improvement. An example is my work with the leader of CSRs (customer service representatives), whose group were taking complaint calls on water and garbage issues in a Florida county. My client had no problem selecting high performers among the 25 persons in this role. A few took less time per call while leaving the customer far more satisfied now that the problem was solved.

I spoke to five persons and learned that their achievement was based on fairly simple factors. First, they knew the contracts with haulers and for water shut off. They did not need to look them up. Second, they were skilled in pulling up two screens—one with past data (eg, complaints, late payments, etc.) and one with the current situation. Finally, they had two characteristics: hustle and empathy. I will not forget one high performer who said that she was sometimes impatient with senior callers who were confused. She said she solved that frustration by imagining it was her grandmother. Most of us have or have had one.

Learning Exchanges

When a staff person at TRI wanted to go to a conference, they did not tell me that it would be a good chance to interact with others or show our flag. They said they had a target of bringing back one new concept, tool, or approach that we could try. If they were presenting, their aiming point was to find at least two groups that wanted to apply something we offered.

This prompted the thought that much knowledge sharing can usefully be seen in an exchange model. It is similar to an import-export scorecard where balance of payments is based on transactions. The group that does a lot of importing, in this case, is likely to grow more than the group preoccupied with exploring its wisdom. Several formats are nicely made to house exchanges and trading. One is a learning bank. On the one hand come deposits—lessons learned, best practices, benchmark findings. On the other hand come withdrawals—persons who take something from the bank to apply. This is one bank where withdrawals can be more plentiful than deposits. The bank analogy can get quite specific, with deposit tickets signifying the presumed value of the entry, and one could have equivalents of checking and savings accounts.

Banking, trading, importing, exporting. These are small structures with rewards that prompt learning. They are the action arm of knowledge, skills, and attributes that trigger improvements.

TRY IT

1. Think of an experience where you learned something that led to thinking or activating differently. Write it up with the Lessons Learned format described and share with another person involved. Ask them to add thoughts then share with a few others.

2. Before you speak with others–whether informally or in a meeting–write two questions you think can usefully guide conversation and give you important information. Ask them, and follow up with more questions until you feel you have explored an inquiry as deep as it can go.

CHAPTER 5

Communicate by Accomplishment

"Results speak for themselves." No, they don't. Someone has to speak for them. Consider two ways of introducing your organization while speaking or in print:

> We are the Bright Horizons Group. We offer enrichment activities to middle school students who are struggling. We have a great passion for helping students read at grade level and know how many challenges they face. We have offered programs to our school district for eight years and are highly regarded. We believe strongly in diversity. We are also research-based, data-driven, and in good standing with all needed certifications.

> We are the Brighter Horizon group. Last year, we helped 320 students who were two grade levels behind in reading get to grade level. This was a 40% increase over the previous year, and teachers say this would not have happened without us.

I have sat through countless openings to workshops and other gatherings where participants were asked to introduce themselves and their organization. When I ask what participants remember after the first few introductions, they typically say, "Not much." One reason is that groups sound so similar when focused on activities. You want communications to help you stand out, not blend in, which means talking about results.

Definition by Achievement

Nonprofits have three ways to define themselves: who they are, what they do, and what they achieve. An experience may help clarify the differences. I was called to the midwest by the head of a state lottery system who wanted more name recognition for his group—and himself. Before I came for a consultation, they had tried the first two definitions. They started with details on who they are. "We are the [State name] lottery. This is our building, our staff, and a picture of our well-dressed director. Here is our mission, vision, and values statement." A brochure was printed and mailed, and a poll was taken. Few cared.

The group then went on to describe what they do. "If we tell the public about our exciting games of chance, that will perk great interest." They did so, with pictures of the attractive scratch-off tickets, and took another poll. Few remembered much. I arrived and asked them to put aside all their research and meeting minutes focused on awareness building, and I asked them to only tell me what they achieved. In under an hour, they had a definition by achievement:

> We are the [State name] lottery. Last year, we made 34 people millionaires and contributed $230 million to our public schools.

People remembered.

While we think of communications as going outward, the most important speaking and writing happens within the organization.

One of the key characteristics of communication that I offer in a course on result leadership is that leaders should talk first and foremost about accomplishment. Here's one of the simulations I use when my participants are in education. I ask for a volunteer to pretend to be the principal of a high school who wants to please the superintendent, whom I play in this scenario:

"Hey, Joe, glad I could drop in. Just a few things of concern. First, the air conditioners don't work in a few English classrooms. I am getting some complaints. Is it fixed yet?"

"No, but it is a high priority."

"Great. And I see the attendance was down at the last two PTA meetings. These can be such a good way to build parent engagement. Can you see how you might encourage more people?"

"Yes, I will. Another high priority."

"Good. And how about those students getting disciplined for putting wet toilet paper in your halls? I am getting some parents really concerned on both sides of that one. Can you resolve their punishment soon? And make sure no one is really upset that it is too strong or too weak. We want to end the year on a high note."

"We will. I'm on it."

"Great. Nice to see you, Joe."

I ask participants if this exchange could have happened in their school. Most say yes. I then ask them if anything is missing. It takes a minute, and someone says, "Yes, there is no talk of learning." Spot on. Indeed, the proverbial person from outer space listening in would conclude that one of the most important priorities in a high school are functioning air conditioners, lots of people coming to meetings, and effectively managing parent dissent. I then model a very different drop in:

Hey, Joe. I wanted to check in on those six students you said were on the cusp of passing Earth Science this term so they could graduate. How did they do on your benchmark exam on Monday?

On the external side, no area has stronger potential for definition by achievement than fundraising. In gradually increasing numbers, some donors want to know the difference they make. Smiley faces, warmth, and habitual repeat gifts are not enough. They want your results, which is a more radical proposition than I would have thought. Many courses are offered on proposal writing where the common expression is "writing a grant." No need to design and implement great projects. All that must be outstanding is the proposal. Chapter 17 covers result-based fundraising in detail.

Informing vs. Persuading

What result do you seek? Any communication needs to answer this question before it is crafted. Many groups, for example, say they want to build awareness of a terrible condition or how our group deals with it. When I ask the nonprofit whether they want people to do anything with their awareness, many say yes. They want them to donate, attend a local meeting, write to their congresspeople, recycle garbage, volunteer their time, etc. This moves the group from educating to persuading as their business. This puts nonprofits in the persuading business. Nonprofits want to persuade people to do something they would not have done before they heard or read what you had to say. Milestones also apply, as in this simple progression:

I am informed: You have given me a lot of information, and I have retained some of it. (But information alone is almost never enough to change behavior.)

I am convinced: I believe I should take action based on what I now know. (But unless they act, today's conviction will be displaced by the new conviction they get tomorrow.)

I am persuaded: I take my first action—then another one. (This is the point of sale. They are not only ready and willing to take action, but they actually do so.)

If you want to inform, you include everything you know. If you want to convince, you want to make a few points in different ways that can prompt most people to form a belief. If you want to persuade, you make sure there are specific avenues for action and a way to stay in touch.

Let's end this section with a critical point. Informers tend not to worry much about where the audience is at. They mistakenly believe that the same messages will work for both the person who is almost ready to act and the person who knows little or nothing about your subject. In persuasion, the messages must get far more personal. When I give talks in an area new to me, I have always called a handful of those who will attend to learn what is on their mind and what keeps them up at night. When I start by sharing what I learned, I leapfrog above the speaker who flies in and out with an assumption that their golden words will inevitably apply.

Results From What You Say

When nonprofits think of communication, they think of their website, brochures, annual report, news releases, as well as comments and pictures on social media. Wordsmithing is often the polish. Does this work? How many people click on that inevitable "Donate Now" button? For anyone focused on accomplishments for those in need, this is a mild mockery. You want me to give money before I get three clicks in to see what you achieved last year? Another drawback to the "read and give" assumption is that people do not give big gifts because they read something. They contribute when someone talks to them.

For every one person who reads something you write, I dare say 10 or more would listen to something you say. Take an organization that has 50 hits to its website that last for 30 seconds or longer in a day. Assume that group has 15 staff and 10 board members, and that each speaks to 20 persons in a day (outside their family and the organization). That's 500 persons, which is 10 times the number of viewing hits. You may quickly say that this is not a good comparison because the board and staff don't talk about the organization with others. Ah, but they could! They just need talking points and time to hone and practice them.

My colleague, Robyn, the CEO of Results 1st, uses a graduation exercise for groups that take part in our project-based program called Result Team Programs. She calls it the Showcase and gets funders present to hear accounts of projects implemented with methods of results going first. She and our result guides tell our groups they have five minutes to cover the following topics:

* Your project in brief
* Its intended results
* What you achieved relative to targets set (numbers, please)
* What you are doing differently to increase achievement next time
* Next steps—where this project goes from here.

When we see a group's first cut at this, many have ignored these headings. We hear, instead, a reminder of how bad the problem is, and what the group did to help others—their programs and activities. We also get self-appointed superlatives. "Awesome experience, amazing staff." This default of starting with need and activities is strongly ingrained in nonprofits. How do you break it? By forcing yourself to say your results first. Start with your targets. Describe your program in terms of what it intended to achieve.

This goes for all your communications, including that huge time consumer called meetings. Staff meetings, retreats, collaboratives, team sessions—so much of our day is spent speaking with others. Meetings do not need agendas of what will be covered. They need a target agenda. "My target is that at least four departments leave this briefing thinking that drone applications could help them, and that at least two take steps to define cost and time savings from a drone deployment." Results 1st has an article on "Results for Meetings." Just ask for it—**info@results1st.org**.

Only one thing is more important in communications than content. It is the person who delivers it. The most ineffective communications I hear are those delivered by talkative people who keep up the words without any useful punctuation. On the other hand, some people are natural communicators and can make even a mundane performance come to life. You need such a person. It may be a board or staff member, a volunteer, or a participant. Find and use them without regard for their place in the organization. A boring or unclear CEO is just another boring person.

Results From What You Write

While we spend too little time preparing for spoken words, we may spend too much time polishing the written word. Visions, missions, website pages, annual reports, and fundraising case books are among the many products that are honed to perfection. Where people disagree, my experience is that they will move to a higher level of generalization where it is very hard to be against what is said. Here's an example from a grant-making group:

Passing Gear philanthropy seeks to engage society's inventiveness and focus its capabilities on situations where current performance is missing the mark. It cultivates the will, imagination, and know-how to enable caring and concerned people to address contradictions between the ideals we hold and the disappointing realities we confront daily.[14]

What elevated language. The problem is the lack of context for either action or confirmation of success. How will we know when we have engaged society's inventiveness? More importantly, what should be different once we do so? We see the same lofty and affirming cast to statements made by CEOs and board chairs in annual reports. I once took five chair reports from five nonprofit annual reports and found that they were perfectly interchangeable. What a way to not stand out!

The same need for clarity of results before you shape spoken content applies to written work. What will prompt people to read our annual report? What do we want them to do or do differently once they have read it? Many nonprofits say that the product is the result: people expect us to produce an annual report, so we do. What an uninspiring reason to spend money, especially on a document I often see few people outside the immediate nonprofit family reading. With web sites I observe an irony in this ubiquitous screen document. The flashing Donate Now button is always on the first page. The results that justify the contribution come much later.

Written thoughts, in most cases, should be as personal as spoken ones. We should say who is doing the talking through words on paper or screen. Many newspapers now do this by stating the names of those on an editorial committee as well as the person who wrote each opinion. With nonprofits, I would like to know if leaders wrote their thoughts or if it was someone in PR or fundraising.

Also, as with speaking, writings intended for internal audiences can be more consequential than what goes out the door to others. In two cases, personal communications really need help to keep a result focus. The first is email. We spend a lot of time on it, and most of that time is spent responding to what others say. When I look at email, my first impression is how few of the messages are linked to defining, tracking, or verifying any form of accomplishment. The exchanges may well provide alignment, encouragement, or another clear message. Given how much time is spent on emails, would it not be of great value if they were used more as means for higher achievement?

A number of organizations have greatly reduced the number of emails they send by applying such guidelines as only copying those who are to do something with what they read. Some have avoided the potential for harm by requiring that anytime a difference is becoming personal, the parties must talk in person. My advice: start every email by stating the result you seek. For example:

> This email intends to give you my candid thoughts on the new program, per your request. My hope and expectation is that you actively consider them.

> This email is to provide everyone at the meeting with clarity on what was decided and who agreed to do what before the next meeting.

> This email is to propose actionable points for us from the recent survey on employee satisfaction. My target is to get comments and additional proposed actions from you.

The standard I like is that the email in some way moves something forward. Many now stay at a lateral point, and a few tend to move the topic backward.

The second mode of personal communication that has ballooned is comments on social media. So many people spend an hour or more daily on Twitter (now X), Facebook, Instagram, etc. While we do so on our personal time, the comments and back-and-forth can readily overlap with work. At the same time, social media can be a big asset when explicitly used in the nonprofit for such purposes as taking temperatures and seeing where people are at before getting into a topic. It is helpful for getting to depth of feeling given that standard filters on forceful expression seem to lower or even disappear.

Made to Stick

This heading is the title of a book by Chip and Dan Heath. I like the way this book defines ways you can make both spoken and written communication memorable.[15] Drawing on this and other sources, here are my top five ways to make communications memorable, which is essential if they are to prompt any action. They apply equally to what you write and what you say.

1. **Keep it simple.** It is tough to sell complexity. "This is complicated. Bear with me for five minutes while I tell you what you need to know." Half your listeners or readers will check out right away. You must get the essence out quickly. One of my favorite quotes:

   "The Lord's Prayer contains 56 words, the 23rd Psalm 118 words, the Gettysburg Address 226 words, and the Ten Commandments 297 words, while the US Department of Agriculture directives on pricing cabbage weights in at 15,629 words." *FN*

   The good news is that speaking or writing about results takes far fewer words than communicating in narrative. The more anyone talks or writes, the less clear they tend to become. Jury members report that in a trial of two or more weeks, the details mush together so much that they rely on feelings and instincts more than data. Before simplicity can apply to the description, it must apply to the content described. When I see a list of 24 objectives (or anything else), I advise clients to whittle this down to the top five.

2. **Add drama.** My granddaughter and I took a boating safety course, and the instructor started by asking for one volunteer. A girl came forward, and he put her in a life jacket, which appeared snug. He asked her to raise her hands over her head. He grabbed the back and pulled it right up and off her. He then noted that he once found a young person who had drowned in only 20 feet of water for just this reason. Wow. He had our attention for the following 12 hours of instruction.

   Animal welfare groups are great at this. I read of dogs and cats that languished in cages for years and faced real abuse who are now thriving in great homes. What prompts me to contribute is not so much the plight itself as the encouraging example of a group helping animals to overcome the plight. The examples did not need great detail or long-winded explanations of mission and vision. Drama is exciting and unexpected.

3. **Be yourself.** Not all of us are at ease behind a podium or a screen that needs to be filled with words. That's fine. We need to find a place where who we are can shine through without forcing us to be different. In general, the direction is toward informal settings. Most of us are comfortable talking with others. I take advantage of that with business leaders whom I have guided. I have spent time helping CEOs who are not great at public speaking to employees

or shareholders. I use an armchair conversation format. I put two easy chairs on stage and open a conversation, drawing out the leader and guiding the discussion of who they are, what they think and feel, and how they view key challenges and opportunities. When time comes to open the discussion to others, it is natural progression.

4. **Watch the PowerPoint.** We are not born scripted. Perhaps the worst form of script is PowerPoint. When a presenter reads their screen, few people stay tuned or even awake. If they do, the content is either so general or so detailed that the audience won't get and keep much meaning. PowerPoint is ubiquitous. If I am speaking to a corporate group, the most frequent question I hear is when they can see my deck. The medium controls the message.

   Other formats can take away energy and insight in the same way. One is the ritual of reading the credentials of the writer or presenter at the beginning of the presentation. An expert before us. I like to wait to draw a conclusion on value until the end, when I know what I have gained. Still another is the inclusion of multiple persons who tell us how happy they are to be here.

5. **Sprinkle in humor.** Humor is leavener. I do not mean the telling of stock jokes, but rather the whimsy and irony that enriches our lives and proves self-deprecating to the speaker. My colleague, Elliot Pagliachio, loved to offer cartoons to accomplish this. One I recall introduced the topic of benchmarking with a slide of a dog irrigating a park bench.

   Another example in my life started with Jim Wooten's column in The New York Times. Jim visited Stump Creek, PA, where we were knee-deep in a self-help project, and called us, "The think tank with muddy boots." I told my wife that I was outraged by the description. "You dumbbell," she said, "That's the best tag line you could have." It was, and was soon translated into a picture of two muddy boots. This brought a smile and made a point.

6. **Suggest what participants can do.** Have you ever heard a presentation or read a report where, after ten minutes, you were absolutely convinced something should be done about a problem or opportunity? The first question at the end of a presentation should ask what a person can do to help. A surprising number of people who are effective at stirring us up do not tell us what to do with our new convictions beyond emailing our congressperson or staying more aware. They did not put results first. The best communications are a springboard, not a conclusion.

I like simple steps that bring the most possible engagement and can be done in the next 24 hours. Focus on personal acts in settings where a response is possible. Writing to a congressperson or other official is very low on my suggested list. High on my list is requesting more information on one of five topics then committing to a 15-minute conversation with a group the writer or speaker represents or knows.

I like taking this a big step further and reducing my audience to those ready to act. For example, I spoke to the North Carolina grantmakers about writing grants to community groups and sparkplugs rather than spending all their money on professionally delivered services. Here is how I organized the 90-minute workshop:

The workshop was split into two sessions. For the first 45 minutes or so, I laid out the community sparkplug approach with examples and saved time for questions. We then took a break, and I asked those who seriously wanted to explore the approach to come back and dig into the details.

About two-thirds of the 40 people came back. I then asked for a show of hands to see who had a serious interest in introducing a small grant program this year. About 15 signified they had serious interest. I put them in one part of the room as the participants from that point on. The res of attendees, I welcomed to listen in. This approach would be extreme if my target was to educate grant-makers on the approach. It was not if my goal was to hit my target of five foundations using this approach.

TRY IT

1. Do a result audit of your website. Start with the home page and note any information present about what your participants have gained from your programs and presence. See how many clicks are needed to get to results. Make or suggest a change to get results to the front.

2. Think of a message you want to stick with people inside or outside your organization. Outline the most critical three points that you see as most important in persuading them to take the action you seek. Review the points noted about stickiness and find ways to incorporate them in each point. Then, see if this works!

PART I NOTES

1. Campus Compact (compact.org) is a national initiative to bring civic experiences to colleges and universities. The practice of equating what a program does with the desired consequences of activity is widespread. I return to this theme in Chapter 16, which explores logic models and theories of change where results following work steps are readily packaged in a diagram.

2. Cause and effect matters. If you assume that low self-esteem (a condition) is the cause of low reading level (a behavior), you might pull students out of reading so they could attend enriched self-esteem building. If you see the arrow going in the other direction, you concentrate on reading first. Most research suggests that self-esteem is an effect, not a cause. One article citing many studies is "Rethinking Self-Esteem" by Roy Baummeister in the Winter 2005 edition of the Stanford Social Innovation Review. If you are prone to setting your results as building self-esteem, empowerment, efficacy, or another condition as the way to help a person develop specific skills, please read that article.

3. The term "BHAG" first appeared in "Built to Last" by Tom Peters and Jerry Porres. I find this book easily as useful as Peter's later bestseller, "Good to Great." It is more powerful than most of the current literature on sustainability because it focuses on what you must build in at the outset. Many sustainability practices deal with raising more money and generating better results at any time in the life of an organization.

4. Macro engineer Frank P. Davidson wrote a highly influential article in MIT's Technology Review called "The case for institutional assessment." His major point was that even large, complicated projects are less likely to work because of a feasibility study than the presence of several highly capable individuals who thought they could achieve something. One of Frank's macro-engineering efforts is the tunnel under the English Channel.

5. Townsend's book, "Up the Organization," is available at many Goodwill stores for a dollar. He was hustling to pull Avis Rent-a-Car even with Hertz. I have used this one for meetings, which can be done in 15 minutes or less—making clear that anyone who needs to sit should do so. I often combine standing with

moving, for example, asking people who have different views to stand next to each other and talk about a solution. A number of books that counter conventional wisdom are full of gems. One I like is "First Break All the Rules."

6. Patton is rare among scholars for his focus on using knowledge. He predates the recent encouraging trend in many universities to hire "professors of practice" who have seen both problems and solutions up close. He writes on the connection of evaluation and achievement: "Evaluative thinking is results-oriented thinking about what results are expected, how results can be achieved, what evidence is needed to inform future actions and judgements, and how results can be improved in the future." Patton wants to help increase results before they are counted.

7. Rubrics are used in education as a scoring guide for writing and other constructed works of students. They clearly state the instructor's performance expectations and are shared with those assessed. Rubrics are also applicable to nonprofit programs where you want observers to use the same criteria to define levels of progress from what they see and hear. This shifts evaluative comments (excellent, poor, etc.) and comparative language (better or worse than) into descriptive language which helps program staff or independent observers to recognize each level of performance with the same criteria.

8. I have sat with foundation leaders who just received their grantee perception report from the Center for Effective Philanthropy. The report lets them compare grantee ratings of all foundations and a specific group of foundations similar to them. Comparative standing is an important metric for any group. I see no equivalent to the CEP for nonprofits. Rating and information systems such as GuideStar (now part of Candid) and Charity Navigator do not use sufficient rigor to see how it compares with other groups on achievement. Most nonprofit awards and recognitions are equally unhelpful if a key criterion is relative gains for participants.

9. Many studies confirm the role of expectations in influencing results. "The Power of Teacher Expectations" (Education Next [Vol 18 No 1]) documents this dynamic that can end with a self-fulfilling prophecy. Sadly, much of the research shows how race, ethnicity, poverty, and gender can prompt low expectations. I much prefer the expectation that all children can succeed. If they do not, the fault is ours, not theirs.

10. So many nonprofits are pushed to define their performance metrics before they have the space to define what success means for their participants or

themself. I always start by asking a group to define success. I then ask them to decide what most reflects success, then how to measure it. If you can characterize success, you can find or develop a yardstick to determine how much of it happens. I have more luck getting people to first say it. Written statements come after that.

11. If you are using volunteers for observation, I like to use images that make sense to them. In this case, the seniors said that spotting those with the highest impact and insight was like mining for nuggets. They said that nuggets shine. We made a list of how they could see sparkle in a participant's response. One way, they said, was hearing the use of strong or unusual words. The instructor was not just excellent, but they were relentless in helping. Another was to look for a level of passion or intensity. As one volunteer put it, when you hear an exclamation mark, take notice. They did not need to learn a new system. It came from them.

12. This definition leads to shifting away from questions on learning to ones that capture a sequence for getting and using information: 1) What stuck with you from this session (or program)? 2) How will you use what you remember? and 3) What difference do you want this change to make? When words take on a result base, the focus changes. Another example is the commonly used expression of capacity building. In a result framework, the point is not to have capacity, but to use it. I much prefer "achievement building."

13. This depressing experience was reported in a 2021 article called "Putting Evidence to Use" in the Stanford Social Innovation Review. The authors speak to how similar conclusions in their group, Innovations for Poverty Action, led them to shift from broad dissemination to forging partnerships with end-users to answer questions most important in guiding their work.

14. I see literally hundreds of such statements from foundations and nonprofits. They all sound both great and similar. In a similar vein, I find it hard to know what a foundation does when its tagline as a sponsor on PBS is that it is dedicated to making the world a better place. Anyone against that?

15. The book is "Made to Stick" by Chip and Dan Heath. Features of content that makes something stick with recipients are "unexpected" and "concrete." Something unexpected just has to be different. The authors note that concrete means you can examine something with your senses. This makes it simple. A great guideline is that you cannot sell complexity. When a nonprofit tells me that, "Our story is complicated," and "Do you have ten minutes?" I am out the door, at least mentally.

Acting Out

One must never speak of feeling to the actor. Search for the life of the part in plans of action, not feelings. Find the action. and the cliches will disappear. If you act and believe, you will begin to feel.

— Constantine Stanislavsky

Learning the five acts of Part I can make you good—even very good. They give you the methods and the discipline to be result-based. This section turns to how to go beyond the fundamentals to achieve breakthrough performances. Each chapter is a practice, not a philosophy. Each can be tried by a small project starting as early as next week.

CHAPTER 6

Keep Your Program Live Longer

Here are two ways to introduce a program:

1. This program is a three-hour workshop offering you information and skills on how to use the internet. Our presenter is highly knowledgeable, and the PowerPoint will be available after the program. When the program is over, we will send you a follow-up survey to get your feedback on the value of the program.

2. We view this three-hour training program as having two parts. Part 1 is on us—we need to offer you information and skills and the confidence to use them. Part 2 shifts to your lead—apply what you learned. We cannot declare this a great session just because we got through the content and you say you like it. Success will be determined in a few weeks, after we know how many participants did something with what they've learned, whether in thoughts, feelings, or actions. We will get your thoughts on what you did in two weeks. Does that sound reasonable?

When a program's ending is defined as the completion of services, everything else is "follow-up." This act is simple and powerful: keep the program in place through an initial period of use. I have used this two-part deal with clients and find that presenters and other delivery staff, as well as their participants, see higher gains. The point is to increase results before you count them.

The Two-Part Program

The period in which participants go home with the knowledge, skills, and confidence to do something with what they learned is your richest opportunity for impact. I have a hundred examples. Here is one: Results 1st worked with a Sarasota, FL nonprofit called Operation Warrior Resolution, which reduces the trauma felt by returning veterans who have been in severe combat situations. The group's signature program had been billed as a five-day retreat with follow-up services. The simple shift to calling this a re-entry success program, which begins with a workshop and continues through application of what was learned, has made a significant difference.[16]

Most participants in nonprofit programs are responders. They take their cues from the program and its staff. Once the delivery part ends, things change—abruptly in some cases. Participants must take the lead to both power and steer their own vessels. The pivot to participant motion is key. As participants graduate or leave your program, one question is critical: Are they activated to move forward without a program to prompt them? That is equally true of programs defined episodically, such as visits to a health care facility. The question after each visit is whether the patient will leave the building and take the prescriptions given—whether it be medication, eating five helpings of fresh fruits and vegetables, or walking at least 30 minutes per day.

When I ask program staff if they can forecast whether a person is likely to take initiative when services end, most say that they can.

They look for two factors: 1) The person really knows what to do and why to do it, and 2) The person has confidence that they can do it, and that it will work. I like an instrument in health called the patient activation measure (PAM). It predicts the likelihood that a person, when they leave a hospital or clinic, will take the needed steps such as taking medicines or other lifestyle prescriptions. Research with PAM has shown that the most influential factor in patients co-owning their own health is the belief that what they do has the power to produce a result.[17]

Part 2 of your program (the shift to participants taking the lead) helps the organization as much as its participants. To begin, it lets you know whether what you did made the difference you thought it would. Consider what can happen after you stop looking:

- The person with a promising job left after two months.
- The person who controlled blood pressure through exercise and weight loss during the program reverted to a sedentary lifestyle within two months.
- The high school graduate who was accepted to college with a great scholarship dropped out after the first semester.

If the program loses track of its participants after services end, it has no ways of changing to alter a potential bad outcome. Many groups use the expression "whatever it takes." This conviction can best kick in during active support to a participant when the script ends and improvisation begins.

These examples of results that did not last are all ones I have seen. I worked closely with the Annie E. Casey Foundation on their Jobs Initiative, for example, and saw many instances where a presumably good job was started, but the participant left. In many instances, the reason given was either, a) the job was seen as a dead end, or b) that the person gained a new supervisor they intensely disliked. Knowing that, the nonprofits began to require some evidence of mobility within six months and support for dealing with a new difficult person. Similarly, I worked with my wife at Green Tech High School as it began to more intensely track its students in the first year of college. They found a surprising number of promising students dropped out—often in the first semester. One reason was homesickness. The students missed family, friends, and familiar terrain now far from their present location. The second was money. They could not buy a tablet—or even a bus ticket home. This led to resources (far less per student than while at Green Tech) and support to handle these challenges quickly.

A second gain for the nonprofit is that it reduces the challenges of staying in touch. I keep hearing how hard this is. Participants move on. They leave the area. Or they stay and lose sight of a program they were told has ended. In my experience, you get three to five times the number of participants who stay in touch when they believe they are still in the program.

Part 2 Essentials

Five elements are essential to supporting participants who apply and hope to continue what they have learned. They continue the rigor of results first and recognize the major difference of supporting a participant who now must be in charge.

1. **Keep up the milestones.** During the program, you defined progress points to know when a participant was tracking to success. Keep them rolling in Part 2. Here is an example of students entering college from a high school college prep program:
   - After the first two weeks, the student is very pleased they went to this school and can see no obstacles preventing them from staying.

- By the end of the first semester, the student is getting at least a 2.0 grade in every class and reports that, in all classes, they understand the content.
- By the end of the first semester, the participant does something with the high school, such as come to an alumni session in person or virtually.
- By the end of the first year, the participant is either enrolling for next year or has an alternative intentional path for success in their lives.

The same conversion ratio discipline applies here as to when the participant was active in the program. In many programs, participant faltering happens soon and can lead to very prompt interventions during this period, just as they did during program delivery. If the student reports challenges within the first weeks, that is the time to respond.

2. **Define an endpoint.** Neither participants nor staff will sustain a relationship forever. Declare a point where Part 2 ends. You can do this by calendar, such as a one-month period to apply what you learned in a workshop, or a two-year period to anchor new behaviors. The guideline I like better is to define a date that is a threshold for predicting longer term staying power. In job development, a period of six months seems to predict that employment will stick. Three months is too short for a good forecast, and two years offers little more accuracy than does half a year. In many cases, the result trail defined in Chapter 1 will offer guidance on a good ending point at which success is either reached or is not likely, at least in a way directly connected to the program.

3. **Encourage peer support.** In many nonprofit programs,

a key factor for each participant is their relationship with other participants or, at least, people who successfully went through the same kind of program experience. For tracking, participants are a cohort. For program success, they are a support group. Shared self-help has long been a critical base for many forms of sustaining self-improvement. Many of us find it hard to act alone and put the greatest trust in people who are going through the same things we are. Self-help groups can have more influence than paid support services. I get deeper into that in the next chapter.

4. **Keep it personal.** The best parts of a program are often relationships with staff and others who connect with participants. At least initially, it may be critical to have the person the participant knows and trusts stay active in at least a "touch base" format. The value of continuity is clear in many settings, including schools where guidance counselors stick with the same class as they move through the grades.

   At times, the relationship endures well beyond Part 2 of the program. I recently attended a session in which the mentors for students who were challenged to complete high school and go to college spoke about how they had maintained relationships over a decade or more. While an end point is important, mentors and mentees are free to ignore it as they pursue additional and longer term gains and mutual fulfillment.

5. **Define the business you are in.** If you say you are in the business of high school graduations or college prep, you stop when students cross the stage and are presumed equipped for post-secondary education. What happens

if you redefine your point to be "college success?" Your former result is now just the launching pad.

This question takes you to your vision. While your mission may be to provide college access, your vision is of youth who go to college and have a great path after graduation. The question also raises core know-how. If one group told me their strength was a great college prep program, and a second group told me their strength was supporting students once in college, I believe I would choose the latter for my kid. What you do well can and often should extend well after your services are "complete."

A broader distinction is worth noting: the shift from helping to consulting. During a program, the nonprofit is expected to be the expert on knowledge and skills and the sequence for acquiring them. During Part 2, however, the role shifts to advising. The best consultants I know view themselves as option-builders. They generate possibilities but do not make the decisions. They are also very sensitive to client readiness and do not advance thoughts that the person or group is not yet willing to consider. The disciplines in Part 1 and Part 2 are different, as are the people great at using them. Core know-how starts with the selection of staff and volunteers for the role that fits them best.

Costs and How to Pay for Them

"We would love to follow up with our participants, but we can't afford to." "Our funder won't give us money to do this." How often do I hear this? Here are three ways to cover the expenses:

1. Know what they are. At the least, see what the cost is before saying you can't afford it. Costs may be lower than you think. One reason is that you move from costs that

apply to all participants to costs that are contingent on someone needing something. Not everyone will require emergency money for bus fare or to fix a car needed to get you to a job or a classroom. You also have participants whom your program greatly helped who will want to help others get what they gained.[18]

2. Show how investing in support costs is the best money investors can spend. If you can get a 30% increase in participants who earn a great gain for only 10% more cost, that is a significant return on charitable investment. This money insures the value of funds spent on Part 1 of the program.

3. Buy the money by serving fewer people. In programs where Part 2 support is critical, starting with fewer persons may lead to better results for more people. This is especially helpful with programs with high fixed costs for each person participating. This does not work if lowering numbers does not lower costs, of course. The point is simply to look at the cost relative to the gain. I return to that theme in Chapter 13.

TRY IT

1. Frame a presentation, workshop, or program with the two-part script defined in this chapter. Watch participants respond and infill support for Part II when they take the lead.

2. Estimate the costs of helping participants get to or sustain success for six months after program delivery. Make explicit your assumptions based on what proportion of your total participants will need different kinds of support.

CHAPTER 7

Find the Sparkplugs

How can you help Cherokee natives, who must transport water five miles because their wells ran dry? That was the question in Bell, Oklahoma, which lies in one of the poorest counties in the nation and is so small that it will never be a priority for an infrastructure grant. The answer: take matters into your own hands.

The Kettering Foundation suggested my nonprofit, TRI, as a resource for the Principal Chief of the Cherokee Nation. Ross Swimmer was very receptive to a self-help approach and picked a water line project in Bell to test its value. TRI guided the resident volunteers to put in a 17-mile water line. They did it. Bell, according to Chief Swimmer, gained a culture of shared capability not by decrying their need, but by solving it themselves. This project was featured in the *New York Times* and a very thoughtful segment on CBS's *Sunday Morning*.[19]

Help From Within

Was Bell a special place? If so, it is joined by over 500 other small towns and urban neighborhoods—from East Baltimore to the hollows of eastern Kentucky—where similar projects were mounted to build and use social capital to solve local problems. Some results:

- In the Peoplestown neighborhood of Atlanta, 20 young adult and teen mothers on assistance gained full-time jobs. Cost per job (through this direct connection of seeker and hirer): $100
- In Oakland, MD, an old downtown building was completely renovated into an arts pavilion by volunteers. During the project period, $45,000 worth of art was sold, and three new businesses moved into empty storefronts.
- In Winston County, MS, 60 tons of trash were removed, and the community purchased an abandoned theater with local funds to turn it into an arts center.
- In Jolo, WV, volunteers converted a closed elementary school into a community center in just three months. When finished, 60 people showed up at the center every Wednesday night to play basketball, and 19 volunteers run programs (including mentoring) for at-risk kids.

These projects were made possible by a nonprofit. Their first role was to help residents believe that they are capable of working together to achieve things. The second role is to guide a process for quickly designing and doing the work. I am saddened that more nonprofits do not pursue this potential, especially since the costs are low. These projects had mini grants made possible by the Appalachian Regional Commission and the Annie E. Casey Foundation. None needed more than $3,800 to complete.

These efforts were not just place-based. They were place-ignited. The spark came from within in the form of one or two individuals we call sparkplugs. Sparkplugs live in virtually every neighborhood or small settlement. They have the stamina and tenacity needed to achieve change without being paid to do so. These persons are far more important than a large committee, a detailed plan, or even plentiful resources. They are also, in my view, the highest form of local social capital. I guided a discussion of 21 sparkplugs who had completed health projects with support from Blue Cross/Blue Shield Foundation of North Carolina. Seventy percent said they got the "bug" of leading projects and went on to do more of them. They are a renewable resource.

There are two key features of this kind of local accomplishment. The first is that all eyes are on results. In the Bell water line project, each work day had a target of how much pipe would be laid by sunset, for example. Each short street wanted to outdo the one next to it. In all these projects, we found that residents were even more interested in getting what they needed than their professional helpers. The only fizzles we had in over one hundred community projects came when the leaders were part of formal planning or development groups.

Residents liked the idea of treating the funder as their investor. With the Appalachian Regional Commission, each project sparkplug looked the funder in the eye and said: "If you make this $3,000 investment, here is what your money will buy." They were clear that the funder and community group needed each other.

The second feature is a personal and shared commitment to achieve the results. I have worked with many groups to write and ratify a compact to capture this. Unlike a Memorandum of Understanding or contract, a compact gains its power as a promise residents make to each other to achieve a result. Here is the Preamble to The Corbett Compact, a document that bound residents of a small and very poor Appalachian settlement to work together on a major renewal project:

WE THE MEMBERS of the Village of Corbett and The Institute of Man and Science [the group I led—later renamed TRI], set forth on an adventure which requires our full cooperation and commitment. Like the passengers on the ship Mayflower, we draft and sign this compact setting forth some articles of common faith and agreement. In doing so, we give our pledge to rebuild Corbett as a small community in which people help each other… in which we can get a good night's sleep… in which our children can range safely… in which we can feel good about our town, our neighbors, and ourselves… in which we do not waste. At the same time, we seek a community in which people live and let live, respecting the rights of others to be different. We want people to grow. Some will grow and stay. Others will grow and leave. But for all of us, Corbett may always be home.

The Preamble was signed at a community dinner by each resident. It was also signed by staff and the board chair at TRI. Our responsibilities were as clearly specified as those of residents. This brought parity in some unseen and humorous ways.[20]

Who's a Professional?

To tap into the capability and willingness of people to help each other, as shown in the examples above, we need to start by tossing out a word that separates people. That word is "professional." It excludes people who can often accomplish the most, beginning with community residents. Many of the sparkplugs that led the eight projects cited above—as well as the Bell water line—did not have college degrees. In fact, some lacked a high school diploma. While we all join in proclaiming the nobility of residents in a setting in need, we continue to cling to the belief that they need professional help to change things. This is an incredibly self-limiting viewpoint.

John McKnight, in a wonderful book called "The Careless Society," makes the broader point that whenever a problem is "professionalized," it reduces the encouragement for people to help each other. Don't you dare provide a sympathetic ear unless you are a credentialed grief counselor. Local communities and support groups are seen as amateurs—well-meaning and hard-working people, but seen at the margins of change rather than the core.

If some people are professionals, others must be unprofessional. One person wordsmiths documents and another cleans toilets to exacting health standards. Who has more value? Why is not every person appreciated for what they do and achieve? Permit me to add another word to the status hierarchy: executives. This term is also a label that separates people. The major certification of fundraisers is called Certified Fund-Raising Executives. Do executives raise more money than non-executives? And we have executive summaries for reports. I guess they are not for non-executives.

These categories may seem benign, but words have meaning that affect not only those outside of the group, but those within it. I once did a project that looked at patterns in the ethical codes of professions and professional societies. One clear pattern was how well they protected and advanced the profession. When we look at job development professionals in communities we see, they look at labor factors and gaps in employment rather than at what is happening in a given community—the 140 people who lack a job in a 10-block area. We define places as zip codes or census tracts, since these are the smallest units of data available, rather than the 140 persons who lack a job in this neighborhood. From the ground, neighborhoods are defined by place names. You learn their boundaries by asking people where they live.

Public and Private Goods

One good way to look at the opportunities of neighborhood power is to see the difference between what economists call public goods and private goods. Private goods, like a house or a car, belong to the owners. Given that the owners get the benefit, they should be the ones to pay for it.

Public goods, like bridges and parks, are shared by many. Simply put, people enjoy the benefits of a public good without helping to create it. Why not let others put in the time or money, since I can use it anyway?[21]

I am fascinated by how much less of a problem this is when you get to ground in a community. For my client, the Seattle Parks and Recreation Department, I studied some community gardens in the city and found that while gardeners took home what they grew, they kept speaking of how gardening built camaraderie among residents, not just for who gardened, but for those who now made the community garden a destination for walks and gathering. The distinction between private and public ownership and gain became far less significant. And at times, it seemed to disappear.

The Cherokee water project was a public good for the residents of Bell, Oklahoma. It was also a private and personal good in a wide variety of ways, such as the pride generated. Here is another: with the blasting and trenching needed to maintain gravity flow, the rule on the water project was that no one could show up who had been drinking. The water line was the big event in town, and many wanted to come and help create this shared improvement. A longer-term gain was the way in which the project helped individuals to gain success, especially in alcohol misuse. Alcohol dependence was so reduced that Chief Swimmer tried to get the Federal government to stop spending money on detox centers to instead simply buy pipe for neighbors to work together on water, wastewater, and housing projects. The response was that this was inappropriate and that a social service delivery system staffed by professionals was needed.

At times, a public group to some is a private group to others. TRI, in partnership with the Environmental Protection Agency and the Ford Foundation, mounted a self-help program in 17 states some years ago. It helped residents put in over 200 water and wastewater systems in small towns. They averaged well over 50% savings over conventional approaches. Why would anyone object to a proposed water line cost of $750,000 dropping to $350,000, which the residences could better afford to repay? Start with the people and groups who received that additional money as a good just for them. Professional engineers are typically paid to supervise projects at a percentage of the system cost. We had to build in great incentives to reduce the price of labor and materials.

TRY IT

1. Identify a sparkplug in your neighborhood or organization. Ask them why and how they became a leader for small change projects. Define the factors that seem to drive them and predict their capability in others.

2. Promote a mini grant program. Ask a board member or someone else who can do it if they would be interested in putting up $2,000 to get one or two small projects rolling.

CHAPTER 8

Try Something Else

Which of these descriptions best fits your organization:

- We are an innovative organization. We not only have a department of innovation and learning, but we also offer a research-based approach to innovation. We have representatives from all departments at our monthly sessions to set priorities for planning innovative projects.

- Last month, we tested five new ideas for doing something differently in an area where we are not effective or efficient. Three of them worked and are now general practice. We have a constant supply of new approaches we are always trying.

Great organizations, very small to very large, have a constant stream of new ideas proposed and tested. They do this by redefining innovation from being about what is new to what is better. They also move from defining innovation as just having a creative idea to actually putting it to use. Innovation, in my result guidance, is defined as the explicit test of a new approach to outperform a present practice. It's this simple: try something new and build on what works.

To try something new, you need a person who wants to do that. We start here.

Critics… Suggesters… Innovators

Three questions for staff and volunteers can get you to innovation:

1. "Can you name an approach or practice in your organization or unit that does not work?" This is the essential starting point. If everything is rosy, why bother to seek alternatives?
2. "Can you think of a better approach or practice?" This takes a pivot from criticizing to seeing an alternative.
3. "Can you design and lead a small project to see if the new approach can do better than how we do this now?" This takes a pivot from advising others on what to do differently to leading change by example.

I see tracking ratios coming on. For every 10 persons in an organization, about eight can answer the first question. This makes them critics. About four can suggest a better way. They can pivot to a suggestion. And one to two will sign up to lead the test of a new approach. They are innovators.

Where do we find them? Most organizations turn to their leadership team. I have a different suggestion. Go to the shop floor where people feel pain from what does not work. Here's an example I experienced. It's 5:30 am at a garage in Schenectady, New York, where the craftsmen for New York Telephone get ready to put up phone and cable lines. One veteran installer became an impressive innovator. Here are his responses to the three questions noted above:

1. What's wrong is that we want to get home for our kids but have three more installations yet to do. This can be solved, but not by the "geniuses" who head the company. The real problem is that it takes too much time. We have

one person holding the ladder, so the top rung won't rock on the pole, and one to climb up and do the work.

2. My approach is to try something I saw on the ladder of a cable company installer. He had rigged the top ladder rung as a V so it would nestle on the pole, and he did not need a second person. He said his company would probably not allow it, so he did the welding on his own time.

3. My project is to put a V on the ladders Tom and I use. I will compare the number of installs we do in a day now with the number we do when each of us can climb a pole.

The craftsman did this, and it worked. The "V" ladder was soon standard equipment and NY Tel CEO Thea Snyder said that this simple innovation project had profound effects on corporate productivity. She noted that it was not surprising that it was the craftsman who had the innovation and desire to try it. She said it would have been far more surprising if she or another executive had the idea, since they did not climb ladders. Email **info@results1st.org** for a link to a short video.

Who's an Innovator?

One of my most reprinted articles began as an article for Chemtech, the journal of consulting engineers. It was called "Assumptions for Innovation," and the first assumption is:

Innovation generally comes from individuals rather than from books, budgets, groups, or other sources. Innovation does not happen when a group removes barriers to prevent it. Innovation occurs when individuals are found and enabled to practice innovative behavior.[22]

In some cases, the innovator is motivated to start a new business. Fred Smith started by trying a divergent approach to package delivery. He leased a few airplanes and tried flying packages into one intermediate point for distribution to many others. That led to

Federal Express. Herb Kellaher had a simple premise that airports could fit in more flights per day by reducing gate time. That innovation started small and became Southwest Airlines.

In most cases, however, innovators are not bold and daring entrepreneurs. They are simply people ready to define and try something new. They come in all shapes and sizes. Some are introverts, some extroverts. Some are older and experienced, some young and new to the organization. Sex, gender identity, position, formal education, age, and most other factors are not good predictors of innovative interest or abilities. What innovators have in common is an itch to act, an openness to very different approaches, stamina to get to the end of a project, and an ability to learn from their actions.

Squelching Better Ideas

Why is the supply and testing of new ideas so low in most organizations? Three traditions in organizations are a good part of the explanation.

1. **The Suggestion Box.** "We welcome your ideas." An employee reads or hears this and submits an idea to the suggestion box, now often in digital form. The reviewer pulls the suggestion out and reads it. Ho-hum. Let's put it on the list for consideration. The flaw is the assumption that energy lies in the suggestion. With few exceptions, the energy lies in the suggester. Here I am. I feel strongly that something should be changed or tried. Until we capture that energy by asking suggesters to become innovators, not much happens.

2. **Brainstorming.** This is a popular way of getting out creative thoughts. We had a conference center at TRI, and I vividly recall one group which came annually for an overnight retreat. The facilitator started off each retreat:

"Once again you have identified the need for more communications and clearer priorities. Let's start with brainstorming activities to improve communication. Just one guideline: You don't have to know what to do with your suggestion. We want to get those creative juices flowing."

Soon, the flipchart or whiteboard was covered with suggestions. The next step was to prioritize them. Physical and digital stickum notes added visual interest and a feeling of engagement.

I took a picture of the brainstormed ideas from this group and compared it with the pictures taken in the previous two years. The list was virtually the same year after year. It did not change because none of the ideas were tested. The reason is that the group owned the suggestions and the group dispersed after the retreat ended. No individuals put their names on ideas as the person who would test their ability to enhance communication.

3. **Supervision.** Most people have a boss, and most bosses see their job as managing or supervising those who report to them. This is more frequently a tight rein than a free rein. When a person goes to their supervisor with a new idea, here are responses we often hear:

   - Thanks. We tried that once, and it does not work.
   - Good idea, but this is not the time to do it with everything going on.
   - We just can't afford it.
   - Let's get a team together to discuss this.
   - I could never get approval for that.
   - Maybe. Ask me next month.

   In each case, the prospective innovators are stopped in their tracks. Here's a very different response:

"We can absolutely pursue this. I love your energy and would like to get you launched to see if that approach works! We may need to make some adjustments, but we can definitely get you leading a small project. Here's a short format to give us clarity on what you want to try and what you think the gains will be."

Why is that so hard? Is it because managers and supervisors have bad values? Far more often, I see this as just bad habits. Habits are ingrained, but they can change with a simple structure like the one we explore in the next section.

Seeding Innovation

Here are the steps in a simple format that move from ideas to projects in short order.

1. Create a sandbox. You get more innovation within a defined boundary than when saying that innovations in all areas are welcome. For example, "We want to triple the number of persons of color who get and use a library card in the next six months."

2. Call for innovators. For example, "We must find a way to be far more inclusive for our library users. We have averaged four persons of color per month in the last six months checking out a book. We want to get that to at least 20 persons per month within the next six months. Do you have an idea to make that happen? If so, please come to this launching session."

3. Get to yes. In a two-hour workshop, you can help innovators define small projects using a proven result-based format. Someone present must then have the authority to modify and approve innovation projects on the spot.

This includes small resource commitments which stop well short of policy or operations changes. Speed is critical to start and sustain momentum.

4. Complete projects. Innovators are given searoom, help, and encouragement as needed. It often helps if their boss or another person is willing to run interference (particularly to act as a buffer from skeptics and naysayers) if needed. If major stumbling blocks are encountered, the external agent pushes for any necessary changes. The date for project completion is held sacred, with an understanding that not all projects will be completed in the two- to four-week period that was set.

5. Learning forum. The price of admission is that the innovation was fully tried. You can learn equally from failure or success. You learn little from a fizzle. The point of the session is to see what's next. This is a springboard much more than a summation. It may be that an idea that kept coming up was finally tested and did not work. Fine, put it to bed and move on. It may be that the gains were strong, and that the practice can go immediately to widespread use. Innovations focused on efficiencies often fall in that category. A third option is moving forward with additional or larger-scale projects that involve more settings, people, and functions.

If you are part of a small nonprofit, you may feel that this kind of process is not necessary. With just a few people, you may think that new thinking and action is ongoing. My experience suggests otherwise. I see many small groups where the familiarity is so high that it is actually more difficult to introduce a divergent idea.

Innovation as Planned Change

While trying better approaches starts immediately and can be intensely local in organizations, it can also use a broader framework of change. The starting point is to see this as a form of research and development. High-achieving for-profit companies hold an assumption that a product starts to become outdated the moment it is first introduced. Competition, new technologies, and shifts in need and context are all factors that contribute to obsolescence. One success predictor is that a significant portion of revenues come from products introduced in the past two years. To make it happen, they invest considerable funds in research and development.

Nonprofits do not have an R & D department. The good news is that they don't need one. In the same way that companies shifted from formal research centers to constant trials of new approaches within each department and team, nonprofits can build product development into refining and spreading small innovation projects that work. The tool to do so is called prototyping. Prototypes—unlike demonstration projects—are done during a design process. Michael Schrage puts it clearly in his book "Shared Minds:"

> The prototype becomes the vocabulary of the innovation, and each successive prototype enlarges the vocabulary and deepens both designer and customer understanding... These rapid prototypes aren't one shot deals: they aren't frozen in final form. They're collaborative learning and designing tools. They're visual and conversational stimuli. They're a medium of expression. You can play with them; turn them upside down or spin them on their axis... They are also highly malleable and manipulable; it's easy to tinker with, edit, or alter them. [23]

Prototypes introduce explicit ways to test assumptions and all factors that are essential to scaling. They are the next step for changes that work. I go deeper with this approach in Chapter 10: Move the Needle.

A broader look at how innovation animates planned change begins with questioning the approaches typically used to make major changes in an organization. A new leader arrives and decides that something should be done differently. They most often turn to one or more of three pathways:

1. Reorganization. Whatever the perceived problems, the fault lies in the present structure. Weeks or months are spent rearranging and renaming the boxes and lines between them on the organization chart. Uncertainties during reorganization tend to sap energy, and if anyone has an idea for trying out something new, the answer is typically, "Not now, we're reorganizing."

2. Studies and Task Forces. In larger organizations as well as in government, further study is advanced as the path to solution. The approach is supported by people who always want more information before they act. The more intractable the problem (think affordable housing, mental health, and climate change), the more another task force or advisory group is required. "We are dealing with homelessness. We formed a task force."

3. Edicts. When reorganizations and studies fizzle, don't worry. Leaders have a fallback: proclamations. Mandates are issued: cut turnover in half, make this division 20% more profitable, require schools to teach to these requirements. If the edict issuer is a state agency or another group with the ability to sanction, they may well get what they require. The bad news is that this is all they will get. Edicts create compliance.

These change strategies are comprehensive, attempting to change many things at once. They are also centralized, reflecting the requirements at the top. Innovation, in sharp contrast, begins locally, focusing improvement on one problem or opportunity. It begins not with theory, but with illustration. It builds on individuals who will lead change by their own example. The good news is that you do not need to spend weeks or months preparing the soil. Your innovators will find a way to sprout.

TRY IT

1. Pick something important that does not work especially well in your organization. Announce and hold a half-hour huddle for anyone who can propose an alternative approach. Ask the proposers who would take the lead in trying out their idea once chunked to a small initial scale. See what happens.

2. Define something your organization now does differently that strikes you as an innovation. Dig in to how it happened and how and why it has or has not worked. Ask what this tells the organization about how to promote change.

CHAPTER 9

Decrease Your Cost Per Gain

Our program has reached 5,000 persons.

Our program directly helped 100 students get to grade level.

Which number is better?

My client, the Freddie Mac Foundation, had two proposals for mentoring middle school students who were behind in literacy. One program said that, for $40,000, they would mentor 400 students. The second said that, for the same amount, they would mentor 100 students. Both would do so for four months. Many donors quickly favor the first program—four times the number of students are helped. The proverbial no-brainer.

At my suggestion, the foundation funded both programs. The program mentoring 400 students had 50 of those students get to grade-level reading. The group mentoring 100 students achieved that gain for 75 students. The overall cost per student, regardless of result, in the first program was $100, and the second was $400 per student. Just divide the program costs by the number participating. If we compare the programs on the basis of what it cost for each student getting to grade level, the comparison reverses. It is $800 for the first program and $533 for the second. If all participants got to the gain, the service and result numbers are identical. At the opposite extreme, if only one person did so, the cost per gain is the full budget.

Introducing Cost Per Gain

You need a way to tell foundations and donors that you are a great investment. This means looking at the level of achievement for the dollars spent. Many tools put results and costs together. One is cost/benefit analysis. An approach that I find more fitting is the simple concept of return on investment, or ROI. It can be just as essential for savvy investors in social programs as it is for financial opportunities. Its value is getting the most gain for the dollars available.

A big advantage of this approach is to let nonprofits ask for the money it really takes to get to a result. The body count favored by some foundations and other donors leads some groups to count the thousands "reached" without the engagement needed to make a known difference. In the example above, the programs were equally efficient. The first one mentored 400 students every two weeks. The second mentored 100 students twice a week. The second had the intensity needed to make a difference. Cost per gain (CPG) is the best way to include program richness.

How Much Should a Result Cost?

What is a reasonable amount to spend to help a person get and keep a family-wage job? What should be the lowest reasonable cost to get a student who is far back in literacy back to reading at grade level? What budget is needed to get a homeless person into and staying in a transitional house? No one seems to know, starting with job development programs, where I see costs range wildly from $1,000 to $50,000 without much variation in job seekers.

It is important for the foundation to know a high return from a low one and to, over time, sort out the highest performing groups in terms of return on grant dollars. As I will cover throughout this chapter, we need to know costs per gain if we are to know how much money it would take to move the needle on a large number of persons with a problem. Without unit pricing, we are just guessing on large quantities of gain.

In business, "industry averages" are vital to determining not only reasonable costs but their relationship to profit margins. In restaurants, the ratio of labor to food costs is key, for example, and in hotels, the cost of cleaning one room is critical information. Health insurance companies are remarkably detailed in projecting the relationship of a dollar spent on prevention to cost of treatment. They know the reduction in insurance payout, for example, for each day increase in the CDC's Healthy Days scale.

In the nonprofit realm, we are now seeing donors interested in solving a problem. They want to know what that will cost. Without some estimate of cost per gain, you have no way of telling them. Another value is seeing how your program stacks up against other nonprofits and their approaches with participants who have the same barriers your participants face.

When I speak of applying the concept of field averages to nonprofits, I run up against two fervent objections. The first is that every nonprofit is different. I was once given a t-shirt by the head of a state association of free clinics. It said: "If you have seen one Free Clinic, you have seen one Free Clinic." I appreciate that all groups see themselves as special, but most of the people and groups that support them want to know how they compare with other groups. The proposition that each is incomparable is not helpful, especially when they all share the same metrics on dollars in and changes in clinical measures out.

The second obstacle voiced is the incredible variation that comes from participant challenges. The cost to help a person, who has a GED and no drug addiction, get a family wage job is dramatically lower than making this happen for a person with a 7th grade education, addiction issues, and other barriers. Variation may also occur due to demographic factors (age, sex, gender identity, ethnicity, etc.) as well as different costs by region or city. All true. Given that the variations are due to known factors, this simply means defining reasonable costs differently for specified circumstances and applications. The definition of participants by level of challenges covered in Chapter 1's section on "Results for Whom?" can help greatly to establish groupings for different levels of reasonable costs. This is not perfect, but can be helpful—especially when a group wants to scale to help many more people.

Decreasing Your CPG

So how do you reduce your cost per gain (CPG) and thus increase the return on investment you offer donors? You only have two paths: increase gains and lower costs to reach them. We have talked about increasing results through the elements of defining, tracking, verifying, and improving the results on which you focus. Broaden your view to ask if you create other gains, whether intended or not. Problems like health, education, environment, and housing are often intertwined. Achievement in one area may be directly and verifiably related to achievement in another. For example, I worked with the parks department in Seattle, which was participating in a prototype approach to seeking investment based on results rather than conventional budgeting. The director realized he produced a gain not generally seen as in the domain of parks. He told the city council that he was also in the education business. He noted that he directly raised student academic achievement by requiring the kids who swarmed to his after-school basketball program to have a note saying that they were not only at school that day, but were caught up on all assignments. When you discover an additional result achieved with very little, if any, additional money, your cost per gain drops and your return on program investment soars.

Now let's look at costs. If a program with a $50,000 budget gets 100 persons to a gain, the cost per gain is $500. If the program can achieve this for $30,000, the cost drops to $300. To achieve that number without lowering the cost would mean getting over 160 persons to the achievement. That is the strong effect of saving money.

You do not need me to help you list all cost control measures. Rather, I select four approaches that are often missed.

1. **Pay more for high-achieving staff.** Nonprofits are admonished to keep their costs down by ensuring they are "reasonable." That means nothing until we connect cost and effectiveness. Take two staff members who are enrolling people in a program at a public event. One is fast and gets 20 people enrolled. Another is slow and gets 10 enrolled. Similar variations are almost always the case. Now let's say that you pay $15 per hour for enrollers. You could actually afford to pay high performers $25 and get a lower cost per enrollment. In many cases, higher priced staff at all levels can get far more done in an hour than lower priced ones. This is also true of consultants. Sure, you can buy the strategic planning consultant for $150 an hour or less, while a brilliant one is $300 per hour. What if the lower cost one helps you to hone and codify your own thinking, while the higher cost leads to a strategy you would never have achieved on your own and doubles the gain that goes into CPG?

While I generally think nonprofit wages are too low, I also resist tying raises to seniority or experience. Tie money to accomplishments such that they are the optimal level to pay, not the minimal level. Increasingly, foundation program officers get this.

2. **Extend the gains beyond the program.** In Chapter 6, we talked about keeping your program in place while people use it. We take up the great increase in returns when you do that. Take two programs that each cost $100,000 and hit their target of getting 100 families to food security this year. Program A used the grant to buy and supply healthy foods through card redemption at grocery stores. When the money to do that ended, the participants reverted to food insecurity. Program B worked with a food bank to connect participants with donated foods and also built backyard gardens. When the program ended, the participants sustained food security through another year. Program B has an annual cost per gain 50% lower than Program A. Email **info@ results1st.org** for a worksheet if the details of this, or other calculations in this chapter, would be useful.

3. **Get to full occupancy.** Nonprofits tend to see their costs as fixed, especially when enshrined in a budget. Overall costs may not vary, but the number of participants over which they are spread varies greatly with one factor. I call it occupancy level, which shows the effects of volume on costs per person. When a group is paying for space and an instructor that could work with 40 persons, but only 20 people have signed up, for example, the added cost for 20 more participants is very small. This is called a marginal or variable cost, and you want to always be close to the

limits of what expensive items like people and space can handle. Optimal size is different from maximum size. If, in this example, you grow to 50 persons, you will have the full cost of a second instructor for the last 10 participants.

Rarely, however, are too many participants the problem. So many nonprofits have programs with fewer participants than expected. This means they are paying for unused capacity.

4. **Buy cheaper.** The best way to get money is to need less of it. A quick look at my bookshelf shows five copies of Dan and Chip Heath's book "Made to Stick" and three copies of Marshall Goldsmith's "Triggers." I will be giving these away to people who promise to read them at my next workshop. Their retail value is well over $200. My cost was 80% less—$1.99 per book at my nearby GoodWill.

Every time a nonprofit brings on volunteers or partners or takes advantage of neighbors and the social fabric described in Chapter 6, they reduce expenses they would otherwise need to incur. This is just about cutting expenses. In the case of local social fabric, it also increases results.

At present, cost per gain is fertile ground for nonprofits because it is so rarely practiced. If you go first and explain this focus to your investors, you can become a thought leader. Better hustle—others who work in your field may go first.

TRY IT

1. Take a stab at computing CPG for one of your programs. Get help from a numbers person as needed and

note the issues faced in this computation. Then compare the cost per person served and the cost per person who gets to the result.

2. Dig into a program with the intent of decreasing cost per gain. Define one action that could increase the proportion of participants that get to the result. Define another that lowers the program costs. Estimate the percent gains in both areas and compute a different cost per gain based on that. Watch your return on investment rise.

CHAPTER 10

Move the Needle

I'm tired of nibbling. What would it take to solve this problem?

More and more, donors ask this question. Few nonprofits have a good answer. While we glibly speak of moving the needle, we do not know the cost, let alone how best to spend the money if we get it. This chapter looks at some steps to take to answer the question then get on with making a major reduction in a malady that has long touched and depressed many lives.

Why Needle Moving is So Difficult

While making a big reduction to a problem sounds great, there are precious few examples of doing so at the scale of even a metropolitan area—let alone a state or a nation. While presidents, governors, and mayors love to take credit for major improvements, when problems lessen, it is typically outside factors, more often than purposeful intervention, that has made the difference. Health is the one area with great exceptions, due primarily to medicines and vaccines. Here are four formidable obstacles to needle moving in such intractable areas as mental health, education, housing, homelessness, and criminal justice.

1. It is tough to add up program results. If one program gets 200 kids to complete homework, another gets attendance up for 300 kids, and a third gets 100 students to rising grades, we cannot add up these apples and oranges. Also, we do not know if these are 600 students, or 400 with overlap in participation, given that some participate in more than one program. Without shared results and metrics, we have no way to connect separate programs. Finally, even if clearly known, the results are often puny. Further, even if we can add up results, the total is often a tiny fraction of those who have the problem.

2. The problem is self-renewing. If a group gets 50 homeless families into transitional housing, a new 50 families may enter homelessness for a net gain of zero. I was always skeptical of the mantra from the federal Housing and Urban Assistance (HUD) that we could end homelessness in 10 years. It proved a major effort in many areas just to keep the homeless number steady over time. In addition to persons new to the problem, those in previous programs that ended may be back to square one. Dealing upstream with prevention that slows or stops the new arrivals to a problem is an essential part of any effort to move a needle.

3. The costs become prohibitive. If the highest-achieving nonprofits need $2,000 to get a person to food security annually, and there are 20,000 persons now food insecure in the geography of focus, the money needed to get them to food security for just one year is $40 million. If that money must continue to help the same people, and new money is required to help those entering the prob-

lem, the amount needed soars in an exponential way. The cost per gain is not scalable.

4. Supply limits emerge. Housing those in need depends on a stock of affordable homes. After an initial period in which all available housing stock has been purchased, the cost of solutions soars with the cost of purchasing and building at largely market rates. In mental health, the problem has already advanced from paying for counselors and therapists to finding them. Solutions at a small scale may simply not be replicable even with enough money.

Size matters, but not always in just one direction. While we like to speak of economies of scale, there are also plenty of examples of diseconomies of scale that show large organizations and programs to be lower performing and more expensive for each person served than in small ones.[24] An alternative to large, centralized projects that tackle "big problems" is a large set of smaller projects that each create great gain for the dollars spent.

The Power to Dent

Whether with a football tackle or solving a social problem, the impact of the hit is not just about the sturdiness of the object, but also the power of the collision. Solutions need to hit problems with some force to make a difference. Here are six promising paths:

1. Chunk down the area served. Senior consultants to the Robert Wood Johnson Foundation program shared with me their approach they used in a national program on youth health. The early results at a population level in the cities of focus were unimpressive. Out of 5,000 youth who had health issues of focus in the given city, a specific program helped 100 in its first year. That's 2%. Now take the

same gain in the context of one school where 200 youth have the problem. That program would achieve success for 50%. My friends called this the Denominator Exercise.

2. Select something—or someone—to grow. Investors have historically spoken of "strengthening the field" and often use this as the rationale to distribute money among many groups. The problem is that not all groups are equally effective, and the cost to bring up the average level of gain is high. The worst way for philanthropy to move a needle is to sprinkle money—even a lot of it. The best approach is to shift from being comprehensive to being selective. This is a hard sell for groups who see nobility in keeping so many nonprofits alive.

    This same logic applies within nonprofits. I find many factors that encourage good feelings about the number of persons now helped. This includes many values statements, which do not need any volume threshold to be seen as present. I look for restive, high-velocity persons on whom you can make an internal bet for greatly increased results.

3. Merge for results. In many instances, I have worked with foundations who see a much higher potential for two or three high-performing groups to work together to achieve stronger results. I will cover collective action in terms of separate groups who work together in Chapter 18. Here, I am talking about a much stronger integration of groups to create a critical mass and tipping points. Larger organizations with more reach and clout may well be needed. This tends to work best when one or two leaders are ready to retire, and leadership of a new group is not at stake. Here's an example:

The leader of the Center for Disability in the Capital District of NY was ready to retire. His choice for a new leader—not surprisingly—was already happy running another group, Residential Opportunities. He approached the ROI leader, and they both thought a merger made great sense. Each group had very different strengths. I suggested that they set aside the mentality of combining—as in, "You have the best residential program, and we have the best business development and workshop program." They agreed and formed Greatness Groups in each area of programs and operations. The mandate: create a new structure that is far stronger than either of the two existing ones. It worked.[25]

4. Look for critical mass. Malcolm Gladwell, in his book "Tipping Point," speaks to Hush Puppies—the classical suede shoes. The company sold 30,000 pairs in 1994. By 1996, it sold over one million pairs. Critical mass is defined as the point at which something (a product, a movement, or something else) gets to self-sustaining change. Part of this dynamic is the diffusion of the innovation curve covered in Chapter 20. Once you get the early adopters, the mainstream will follow. I worked with a community development corporation (CDC) in the 9th Ward of Houston. This group had used a scatter-site approach to exterior home improvements with the hope that when one home was fixed up, others in a neighborhood would follow. They changed to a concentrated approach within a two-block area. The CDC found that once they had three homes spiffed up in that small area, it

sparked a tipping point to many others in that immediate area. Tipping points for community change may need proximity more than mass.

5. Use existing delivery systems. My client was a national foundation focused on social determinants of health. They wanted to support programs that could show a direct connection between healthy fruits and vegetables and better health. They received applications from nonprofits who wanted to create new delivery systems at very high costs. Instead, they found a few Federally Qualified Health Centers (FQHCs) who wanted to integrate food security with their clinical practice. They viewed fresh and frozen fruits and vegetables as prescriptions and provided a number of supports for patients to take this "medicine." The cost per gain was dramatically lower given that they already had patients, facilities, and delivery staff.

6. Build a franchise. The strategies above are largely bottom up. Start with individual groups and build larger structures and programs. An approach with equal value has a centralized starting point. Someone builds an effective enterprise then replicates it in many places by offering franchises to people who will use that approach. Franchises have two key features. First they completely define what has to be included in each place for the approach to be successful. A playbook is provided. Second, they tap local innovations. McDonald's reports that many of its new food selections and store layouts were tried and tested by franchises. The for-profit franchises that ignore this resource—including some private school alternatives to public education—do not fare well in my experience.

While we think of this as a business model—from hamburger chains to exercise centers—it is just as relevant to dealing with social problems. Without this logic, the so-called quest for national models and best practice often end with local programs that have to reinvent wheels almost daily to get things done.

The Big Bet

While franchising is a combination of centralizing and decentralizing forces, the big bet is intentionally top down. It typically starts with major money, almost always from outside the setting. A national example is philanthropist Walter Annenberg who stood in the Rose Garden in 2014 and said he would put up $500 million to, "guarantee our nation's future by covering the cost of reform in thousands of schools." The grant raised an additional $600 million and reached more than 1.5 million children in over 30 states. Assessments have concluded that while the initiative had a positive effect on some schools, it did not gain the traction to change systems or outcomes nationally. Other efforts have focused on states. The Gates Foundation spent over $100 million in Texas and California to reform high schools, with results from the new, smaller high schools not substantially different from the unreformed schools.

An example takes us down to one urban school district. In 2009, Mark Zuckerberg, founder of Facebook, committed $100 million to raise academic achievement in Newark, New Jersey. At that time, 95% of Newark students were black or Latino, and 88% qualified for free or reduced lunch. Forty-four percent lived below the poverty line. Set against these forces was a stellar cast of reformers with the power and intense desire to help make a difference on the ground. Senator Cory Booker was the then Mayor, and Chris Christie was the governor. They brought in a reform specialist, Cami Anderson, as the new superintendent of schools.

Results fell far short of promise. When test scores for 2014 were known, all but one of the schools that had been designated as in urgent need of renewal had seen scores drop in literacy, math, or both. Of equal importance, the city and school neighborhoods voiced great animosity. The initiative by many measures had a net negative impact. What went wrong with this big bet?

My insights on that are largely taken from an insightful book, "The Prize" by Dale Russakoff. She offers an eye-popping look at what happens to derail the best of intentions based on the best reform principles. Six factors emerged for me in reading the book and speaking with Dale.[26]

1. The money needed to solve the problem was never computed. "Booker asked Zuckerberg for $100 million over five years. The mayor conceded, however, that he did not know at the time what the initiatives would cost. He chose the number largely for its size and the public attention it would draw to the effort."

2. The key roles were not clearly defined and generally came from outside Newark. "Anderson's gale-force advocacy for her point of view was a major asset, given the baffling lines of authority among Booker, Christie, and the philanthropists." Many consultants, largely White and from out of town, were paid money for assessments and advice.

3. Competing interests, most anchored in the way things had been, were formidable obstacles. "Redirecting large district bureaucracies—for decades the employers of last resort in distressed cities—in the service of children in classrooms is a treacherous process, activating well-organized public workers, political organizations, and unions invested in the status quo."

4. Existing contracts were not understood. More than $60 million was spent to cover the cost of low-performing teachers who were pulled from classrooms, but who still needed to be paid. That alone was 30% of the full $200 million. Also, union contracts barred teachers from non-teaching tasks such as spending break time with children who needed to calm down. When layoffs were needed in the project, high-achieving teachers could be kept only if they had the most seniority.

5. High expectations were constantly stated and streamed in from national groups and programs. "Transformation was a popular word among education reformers. Teach for America promised 'transformational teachers;' New Leaders for New Schools, 'transformational principals;' the Broad Center, 'superintendents with transformational skill who would enact transformational sustainable and replicable reforms.'" When residents read and heard such sentiments and saw no real change on the ground, the distance grew between vision and reality.

6. The cumulative effects of poverty were not fully addressed. Overall impact of trauma, health, housing, and street violence are stark influencers of educational attainment. The program appeared to have an assumption that educational gain could surmount these many problems without massive help from health, housing, and social supports.

It is one thing to place a small bet for an improbable but huge return, as lottery ticket buyers do.

It is quite another to place a large bet with unknown and often very low returns. Certainly, big-time money is not a fast highway to solving tough social problems. You may think of Newark and other large initiatives as irrelevant to a group with a budget of $100,000 or less. Think again. Small groups also make big bets relative to their size. We may spend all of our available money on a new program or a new staff member. Just the fact that this precludes spending in other ways makes it a significant bet. Further, all of the six points gleaned from Newark apply in one way or another.

TRY IT

1. Note the number of persons who have achieved the result you set. Calculate the percentage this number is of the total who have the problem in the geography you serve. Now ask how much lower that geography must be such that your success number is 25% of the total in need.

2. Think of the most ambitious initiative which your non-profit has ever mounted, even just considered. Note at least two of the approaches defined in this chapter that would have raised the gain or lowered the cost. Starting with a small change is fine. It adds up when you work both factors.

PART II NOTES

16. "Are You Terminal?" was my blog entry of April 13, 2022, which describes this project with thoughts from the nonprofit leader of this story. You can read this or other entries by clicking "Hal's blog" on the website www.results1st.org. The blog is a small example of a technique to help ideas come alive through whimsical graphics.

17. For more information on the Patient Activation Measure and its uses, see the recommendations section in my study, "The Great Community Health Center," published by the National Association of Community Health Centers. It is included in the Results 1st website section for book readers. The instrument was developed by Judith Hibbard at the University of Oregon and holds promise for gauging participant activation in many areas, including education and both food and financial security.

18. I attended a 2023 program in Florida that featured mentors in a college prep program called Take Stock in Children Manatee. Most had been students in the program who wanted to pay back the gain they had received. They said this did not seem like a charitable act. They said that the feeling of giving was overwhelmed by the experience of getting. A great deal of research finds this perception widespread. Those who give time feel less time pressure and believe they are more "time affluent." A Google search will get you to these and other findings that dispel the adage that time is money. It can be more, especially for persons who know what a role takes to help someone like themself.

19. This "Sunday Morning" coverage includes resident comments. They are clear and literal. Woodrow McChrisian, who worked every mile of the pipeline, said this on the Charles Kuralt program: "I believe in just this knowledge of knowing that people can still help each other. In place of big me and little you. Seems like about 99% of the world anymore has got to I got mine, you go get yours."

20. The Corbett project had a research component. One researcher put in a question about income. The first time the researcher asked about money, a resident replied, "Sure." But first, how much did you make last year? The compact

had one simple line: no researcher can ask a Corbett resident any question that the resident cannot first ask the researcher. The question disappeared. Such simple statements can achieve more parity than detailed memos.

21. An academic look at this challenge first appeared in a book by Mancur Olson called "The Logic of Collective Action." He wrote: "Indeed, unless the number of individuals in a group is quite small, or unless there is coercion or some other special device to make individuals act in their common interest, rational self-interested individuals will not act to achieve their common or group interests." We found his conclusions accurate and needed ways to connect private and public interests in community renewal projects. One was to sequence residents buying the house they had rented after the completion of the water line, sewer line, or other shared goods. In another project, residents chose to charge persons who did not contribute their share of Saturday work hours the dollar equivalent. This greatly reduced resentment toward those who went fishing instead.

22. "Assumptions for Innovation" first appeared in Chemtech, the journal of consulting engineers, and is among my top five reprinted articles. One reason, I think, is that the assumptions are short and followed by a response to the "So what?" question. If this assumption is accurate, what should it lead you to do differently? I deleted about five initial assumptions because I could not think of a use for them.

23. Schrage published "Shared Minds" as a study in collaboration in 1990. He has stayed and built his insights for many years. I particularly like "The Innovator's Hypothesis" published in 2014. Its tagline: How cheap experiments are worth more than good ideas. "Quick and dirty" for prototypes may also be called fast and clean. Dirty means murky when it comes to seeing early-on if an assumption holds up.

24. In 1982, Kirkpatrick Sale wrote a widely quoted book called "Human Scale." In 2017, he published "Human Scale Revisited." Sale presents a good deal of evidence for both efficiency and effectiveness by bringing human enterprise back to a scale we can comprehend and manage. One theme is decentralization. He notes that while corporations keep growing, their units of production and design get smaller—whether in producing steel from specialty shops or printing books once they are sold.

25. Nonprofits should look at merger potential more often than they do. Three factors block this inquiry. First, they quite rightly see morale dropping in

merged organizations. Second, leaders each want to be assured they will be on top in the merged group. And third, nonprofits—especially boards—cling to fierce independence. "No one can do it like we do." In the case of these two nonprofits in the field of developmental disabilities, the focus on creating a great new organization led to staff and board reporting an actual boost in morale. Little effort could be spent in the conventional quest to see what place a person would occupy in the new order since it had not yet been created. The "Merging to Greatness" case study is in the book readers section of the Results 1st website.

26. "The Prize" is an eye-opening study of a big bet that seemed to have all the ingredients, yet fizzled in achievement. I see so many of these factors repeated in many large projects. The hardbound edition's 218 pages are a way to benchmark a fizzle without leaving your chair.

Pivots in Formats

I am no longer accepting the things I cannot change. I am changing the things I cannot accept.
— Angela Davis

Many organizations can utilize books and consultants to elevate the conversation to matters such as values, beliefs, mission, vision, aspirations, and the transformations to get there. In my view, they miss the one factor that most shapes behavior: our formats. These quiet and widely accepted ways of putting things together have outsized power to govern what we see and often what we think and do. They seem like tools but come packaged as our structure and process.

This Part explores my seven favorite formats, each a verb which leads to a noun. For example, planning leads to a plan, budgeting leads to a budget, and organizing leads to the org chart. Nouns and verbs are often interchangeable. Traditional formats are fluid in words but operationally rigid, which is one reason they are attractive.[27]

We do need a way to characterize the structure of the organization and the nature of individual roles. We do need logic to connect what we do to what we achieve. We just need pivots to different approaches and formats that tie directly to success for those you serve.

I like the term pivot. In sports, it means moving one foot while keeping the other planted as a push off. A pivot is also defined as, "a shaft or pin on which something turns." It can put results at the center and supply the leverage for all revolutions.

CHAPTER 11

The Organization Chart: From Boxes to the Spaces Between Them

The picture is clear: a set of boxes connected by lines. Over here is finance, and over there are operations and programs. Everything has its place. While funders may require it, the organization chart seems of very little use operationally. At least half the time I ask to see one, the response is that it is outdated. Rarely is it considered obsolete because of any change in structure. It simply needs an update of persons. The pieces prevail. The product is stationary.

For all formats, the real question is what contribution it makes toward accomplishment. If a group performs at an equal level with a great chart, a bad chart, or no chart at all, what's the point?

How Org Charts Depress Achievement

A pattern throughout the seven formats I explore in Part III is that they all take the eye away from results. We depress achievement not by ignoring conventional wisdom, but by following it. Here are four ways in which the organization chart makes it hard for results to flourish:

1. **The portrait is of hierarchy.** The CEO and other leaders are on top. Down the chart are directors, managers, supervisors. At the bottom are those on the shop floor, including those directly interacting with customers and keeping the floors clean. Levels differentiate status as well as compensation. Authority in the charts of larger organizations is reinforced by expressions such as "chain of command." Leaders are thought of as individuals, those in the middle as groups, and those at the bottom as a workforce.

    The effects of hierarchy are strongest at the lowest level, where the full weight of the organization falls upon the occupants. While those directly interacting with clients are most often the key to participant success, they are paid the least. This is also true in many corporations. Tellers are the key to the profitability of bank branches. Most of us are more taken by the teller remembering our name than by anything written by the branch manager.

2. **The components are distinct.** Like a jigsaw puzzle, each piece has only one right location. Innovation belongs in the department of learning and innovation. Results are housed in a department of evaluation or data analysis. The org chart screams of separations. They begin with departments and other boxes, but are readily absorbed up by the persons who occupy them. Thus, persons are asked to attend meetings to "represent" another department. While tempting to think that this and other challenges only exist in large organizations, I have seen plenty of nonprofits with a three- to six-person staff where distinctions such as "finance" and "programs" lead to separate allegiances.

    When components are fiefdoms, one challenge is that each can maximize performance in their area in ways that fall far short of optimizing anything. This is aided when leaders provide little or no incentives for collaboration among units.

3. **The flow is largely downward.** Two words reflect the ways in which information moves in the hierarchy. One is "cascade." The top line goals cascade down to intermediate and lower levels. This is assuredly comforting because the explanation for this happening is gravity. The other term, "roll up," reverses the direction and must push against natural forces. When I talk to leaders about what has come up to them from the lower levels recently, I often get little response. This can happen in very small organizations. If you work for a leader in a two person group, how often do they listen to you or share what happens at their level? You do not need to print a chart to feel the effects of one.

4. **Value lies within the boxes.** This, in my view, is the biggest shortcoming of the org chart. Great effort is made to position functions and roles between departments. There is little attention to synergies, collaborations, and other connections among boxes. Visual explanations are sometimes used to depict overlap. Here, for example, is the great circle route:

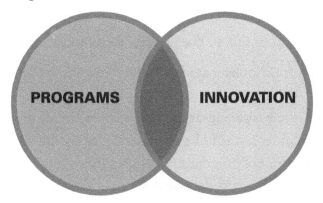

A visual on overlapping interests says nothing about mutual engagement.

My eyes caught a passage in a newspaper article recently that spoke to how and why the Centers for Disease Control and Prevention (CDC) seemed to be lagging, rather than leading, during the COVID-19 pandemic. Rochelle Walensky, the CDC director, wrote:

"Yes, we are going to be moving some boxes around on the org chart. However, I cannot stress enough that moving boxes around will not modernize this agency or prepare us better for the next pandemic. Changing culture will."[28]

Part of the separation is created by the persons typically seen in different departments. Some CDC boxes contain scientists and academics. They are cautious and want a lot of information before acting. Other boxes contain people who deal with the media and politicians. They have a strong need to show decisiveness and lose ground every time they have to say, "I don't know." Still others are public health practitioners who believe that imperfect knowledge is enough to get going. How the persons in these boxes relate to each other to achieve stronger results determines culture. In fact, it is the culture.

From Boxes to the Spaces Between Them

The pivot is from looking at what happens within the departments and units to looking at the rich terrain of interactions among them. Start with the basics and ask each department and unit what it needs from other boxes to be as successful as possible. For example, a department of programs needs help from:

* Assessment and data analysis to show the results of

their program needed to get more money

* Innovation to create a flow of new ideas tested to improve performance
* Finance to show return on investment and cost per gain
* Human Resources to hire new people based on the factors that most predict success in a role

These relationships start as transactional. We help you achieve your results, and you help us achieve ours. It's a start. To sustain this, leaders must provide incentives or requirements. "Part of your result for the next six months is to show that you requested help three times and responded with help three times." Even this minimum does not come naturally. I have worked with three governors and their cabinet or sub-cabinet to see how strongly each looks to position their own success as separate from that of other departments.

The more powerful form of interaction goes beyond exchanges to shared ownership of accomplishment. The word I like is "collaboration," and it focuses on how two or more actors can achieve something together that they could not reasonably have accomplished on their own. You will find much more detail on this in Chapter 18. Here are examples:

* The health and education programs of a nonprofit decide that they should co-locate their service locations. They co-own, making them as successful as their participants see it.
* Three departments co-invest in a new project management software they believe can cut time by 25% with no loss in results. They ask the staff lead to work for all three groups creating it.
* The innovation fund managed by one department makes small investments in five different opportunities

in five different units of the organization. It declares it is fully dependent on other departments for return on these investments.

How do you show this on an org chart? Just make room to list the top interactions right on the chart.

New Visuals for New Meanings

Pictures give as much or more meaning than narratives. Here are four ways to approach visual explanation of an organization.

1. Go from portrait to landscape view. How would we work if we had fewer people in the middle? Create less distance between the top and the delivery and much more space latterally to explain relationships among the units going sideways on the chart. This shows that those on the shop floor have a clearer view of the top and fewer persons in between to say no.

   In this and other possibilities, start with questions. What would our school district organization chart say if principals reported directly to the superintendent, with the leaders of curriculum, discipline, and other areas depicted as support services to that simple two-level hierarchy. Just play with it to see what visual explanation might yield.

   A common concern is that without supervision and management, this flattened organization will lose control. This need not be the case. They shift from control of activity to control of results. If you know and approve what each staff person is focused on achieving, your main job is to help make that happen.

2. Reverse the top and bottom. A bolder view suggests upending the org chart. One exercise I like is to imagine

the triangle inverted. How would you draw it if those who touch participants were on top, and the leader were on the bottom? I see this leading to fascinating conversation about how information flows and stated results for each level that explicitly contribute to organizational goals. Another possibility is to add your participants to the top. Why are they not part of the organization? It is hard to imagine them placed next to leaders with whom they do not interact. It is much easier to see them next to and above those who directly help them. Another way to play is to draw an hourglass. At the top, the wider dimensions give room for leadership teams, rather than individuals. The middle is thin, and the bottom widens to where change generally happens.

3. Show relating, not formal relationships. The organization chart is designed to override the idiosyncrasies of individuals to show the constancy of roles and distinctions. The richer path is to depict how individuals within a box move among them by personal inclination. My favorite example of this comes from a song and story by John McCutheon called "Christmas in the Trenches." In the first World War, British and German soldiers facing each other across no man's land started singing and interacting on Christmas Eve. How about a chart that follows the unit leaders from a department traveling to other places on the chart where they can be most helpful to organizational achievement. Movement starts with people who move.

4. Try a circle. See what happens when you put leaders at the center and use concentric circles that move out to program delivery and customers. I have seen the spatial

layout prompt great conversation on how lines of communication flow around the circles without needing to go upward. Anything that offers a new starting point can suggest new modes of thinking. Being "on the top" versus "at the core" certainly suggests a different role and, perhaps, even a different purpose.

TRY IT

1. Draw a new figure–reversal of top and bottom, hourglass ,or something else. Fill in just a few key locations and ask a colleague to ponder with you what the organization would be like if this were its shape. Stay open!

2. Meet with a person in a comparable role from another department. List three ways each of you has knowledge, skills, and targets that can add value to the other. If that works, do one thing to help that person achieve more. And ask for the same from them.

================= CHAPTER 12 =================

The Job Description: From Describing the Role to Defining its Achievement

---

This is a written description of your job. You will supervise these people, perform these functions, coordinate with these teams and initiatives. Your authority and responsibility is prescribed, and you are located at a level depicted on the org chart. Are you clear on what you are to do? The one thing missing is what you are to accomplish. How many people do you know who are excited by their job description?

How Job Descriptions Depart from Achievement

Here are four ways this happens. Job descriptions:

1. Focus on what a person does rather than what they achieve.

    For example:

    * Serve as primary liaison to IT regarding student success software platform
    * Revise and expand co-curricular offerings

169

- Implement recruiting and outreach programs
- Supervise all library staff
- Lead team in updating strategic plans

Nothing is said about how many people are to be recruited, what library staff are to achieve for patrons, or what the strategic plan should do to increase performance. Rather, "do your job" is the premise.

2. They inhibit collaboration. People do not need help to do their job. These are my duties, and these are yours. They are separate. But they do need help to achieve a result. Job descriptions make that difficult by separating roles. Most staff say they believe in teamwork. Where, then, do you read a job description that links two persons to the same accomplishment?

3. They encourage hiring at the average. When we read job activities, they all sound the same. Little, if anything, sparkles or shows great success. Further, applicants will be almost certain they can do the things specified. They can readily "fill the position." No focus is on getting world-class people, and no self-selection is possible from applications who may best know what they can achieve.

4. They drive performance reviews to the ground. We see formats for rating employees with terms such as "met expectations." What a low bar, since the expectations were about performing functions with little regard from what was achieved—especially for the participants the nonprofit is there to help. If you were expected to supervise five persons and did so, you have met, if not exceeded, expectations. Routines are rewarded. People stay in their lanes.

From Describing the Role to Defining its Achievement

This pivot is not difficult to see:

Job description: Director of Training and Development:

Responsible for all training programs for the 450 persons in the department. Supervises staff of five and reports to Senior Vice President for Human Resources. Duties include:

* Design and deliver courses on a full range of supervisory, management, and leadership topics to include effective communications and team collaborations.
* Evaluate all training programs through timely surveys.
* Responsible for maintaining all training records and expense reports and ensuring that costs are within budget on an annual basis.

Result description for the same position:

Responsible for ensuring that all staff believe they have the support to grow and achieve at a high level. All feel a high sense of belonging and achievement.

* Participants in all training programs will report—with examples—how the program tangibly improved their knowledge, skills, and organization.
* All staff with your support develop and pursue for each quarter a learning target for personal and professional improvement. They take initiative and get the support they need to achieve it.
* Employees and their managers will have and use a format for knowing where they stand with each other on a monthly basis.

Result descriptions have four huge advantages. Result descriptions:

1. Define success as the value others get from what you do. When we shift from focusing on what a person

does to what they achieve, we invariably bring in customers. These are the people who use what we produce. The customers for financial reports are those who can use those reports to change what they do to hit budgets. The customers for a manager are those they manage. The customers for a workshop presenter are the participants there. The result is to give them great value. This leads to invaluable conversation with your customers, asking what they need in terms of speed, content, or anything else that increases your value to them.

2. Compel collaboration. If a person has an ambitious target, chances are good they need help to achieve it. I like result descriptions that actually build that in. "Here is what I need from three other people. I've included their agreement to provide it." This alone is energy building. People like to be helpful to others, if for no other reason than to show their value. They like being asked, rather than told. When I ask most non-profit staff if their organization believes in teamwork, everyone says yes. Let's give them a format that enables that to happen. Results do not just encourage collaboration, they require it.

3. Provide aiming points. While the results may not vary over time, specific levels of results, called targets, are best stated as time-specific. For example:

   "In the next 12 months, I will ensure that at least 300 of our 450 staff can not only specify the skills they have learned, but can show evidence of how those skills led to higher performance. In the second year, this will rise to 425 of 450."

   "In the next six months, we will reduce our waiting

list for the program I lead by 25%. In a year, it will be gone. I will spearhead an all-out mobilization of the four people staffing this program."

When I ask those in an organization if their jobs fit with other jobs, most say yes. I often hear that jobs are aligned. What a weak word. I don't want to know that jobs are distinct, compatible, or coordinated. I want to know that they spark achievement in each other. The last thing I want to hear is that jobs are mutually exclusive.

4. Put achievement first. If a person has a specific target, the focus is different. "Here is what you said you would achieve in the last six months. Did you achieve it?" If a person did not achieve their result, the explanation may be that they did not get the help they clearly needed. "I am clearly involved here as your boss. What should I have done to help you? I want to do that in the next six months."

Result descriptions get a big boost when we pivot from what we do to what others get from what we do. All of us have customers in one way or another. Start there and include:

- Your customers (by name if possible) and what they need from you
- What it takes to make each customer group highly satisfied with what you provide
- The help you need as a customer of others
- The two specific achievements that are most important for you in the next six months.

We can provide a format and a workbook to you. Request at info@results1st.org.

1. Write your own result description. Don't make it complicated. Just state the top three specific accomplishments that most define your success in the next three or six months. Do this in two domains: what you think your boss and leaders most desire and what you personally believe is most important. If different, figure out a way to raise that to get aligned.

2. Make a list of your top three customers–those inside or outside the organization who most need something from you. Use names, not categories. Now write what you must produce to make them raving fans of your help. If you are not sure, interview them. Then, make sure at least one customer high-satisfaction achievement is on your result roster.

CHAPTER 13

The Budget: From Money in Categories to Costs Accounted to Achievement

When I ask people what the point of a budget is, they generally say it is to define and control costs. Almost never do I hear that the point of knowing costs is to make sure the gain is worth the expense. Funders join in this control mode by asking for an explanation of any variance between budget and actual costs that is more than a certain percentage. More people ask for the size of the organization's budget than the size of its results.

As with other formats, the effects of this one are large. We isolate money, for example, not just in programs, but in people. When we ask if this is a reasonable salary to pay a CEO, we assume that cost can be separately considered. In reality, the salary listed is probably too low if the leader has created a booming enterprise with gangbuster impacts, but it is too much if the person is struggling to keep the nonprofit afloat.

The separation of costs and gains reaches absurdity when the government uses a practice of separate submissions in a grant application—one a technical response and the other a budget. These are then reviewed and given points by different reviewers. A relationship of costs and gains is precluded.

Finally, separating money and participant achievement eventually divides the persons who do these functions. Finance folks are "bean counters" and program staff never think about what it costs. All told, the effects of the budget as a standalone format are very significant.

Budgets define money at rest. When spent, it is noted to track expenses by category. This form of cost control tells you the total you have spent. It tells you nothing about what the money was spent to do, let alone achieve. We need a pivot to get there.

From Budgets to Cost Accounting

The pivot is from tracking expenses to seeing what they buy. This is the discipline that tells you what each activity costs and enables you to compare the cost with the gain achieved. Let's start with knowing what things cost. If you do not know that, you have no way of looking at cost relative to gain. Nonprofits rarely know this because they do not pull money out of the budget and allocate it. They rarely know the cost, for example, of strategic plans, retreats, or other internal activities that consume time and other expenses. When I ask for the cost, I am usually given the expense for the consultant, the off-site venue, the printing, and other expenses. This ignores over 80% of the typical cost, which is time. Assume that 10 staff are involved in five meetings, including prep and follow-up time to complete a strategic plan. Assume an average time spent of 80 hours. That's 800 hours total. Assume that the full cost of those 10 persons (including taxes and all benefits) was $70 per hour. Now add the time that leaders spent working with the board and getting the plan to the website and other places—say 20 hours each for two higher-salaried persons at $100 per hour. The total for time is $60,000. Only when we know the costs can we ask if the envisioned gain is worth it.

I first learned how to do this kind of cost accounting at TRI, which had a conference center. We were competing with other venues for business from New York State agencies. One competitor charged $140 per night for room, meals, and conference spaces and was a two-hour drive away. Our center was an hour drive, and we charged $175. Here is the point we made: Fifty persons at $75 average cost per hour totals $15,000 time cost using our competitor. For our conference center, it was $7,500. We were by far the best option when all costs were included. A pause to listen: I can hear a reader saying that time is not really a cost since we have to pay staff in any event. My response is that if there was nothing else of value they could have been doing, they should not be there at all.

Once you know the costs of something—whether developing a plan or getting participants to show up for the first session—you can take steps to compare cost relative to gain. Here are four applications I find critical:

1. Seeing net performance. Financial investors are not overly interested in costs or revenue as separate items. They are interested in the net when costs are subtracted from revenue. With nonprofits, the cost per gain (CPG) in Chapter 9 is a form of cost benefit analysis with the gain put in non-monetary terms. A special use of this kind of format is with activities whose value is seen as an article of faith. Companies for years spent a large amount to send executives to professional development courses. How could one not get much more proficient having attended a Harvard or Stanford program? Now the question is whether the $10,000 spent will add enough value in increased productivity and morale.

2. Investing instead of budgeting. Historically, organizations are asked once a year to do a budget to define their spending. Groups have to justify budget increases due to rising expenses or higher costs. I like the shift from spending to justifying money on the basis of return. Here is what we commit to achieving next year, and here is the money it will take to do it. The focus moves from line item scrutiny to the overall relationship between money and gain. I find this far more energizing, especially with the opportunity for higher investment. This is the opposite of a budget increase of 5% for every unit. This also works within organizations using an investment request template.

3. Understanding cost changes with size variation. "What are the costs per person if we have a 25% increase or decrease in participants? What if we could complete the program cycle either two weeks faster or slower?" Financial projections allow for "What if?" questions that can lead to knowing where you should concentrate so you can decrease cost per gain. Some formats that have been honed for decades in business can help as well. One is called breakeven analysis. "How many of this product do we need to sell so we cover all of our costs?" Find the number of participants to cover the costs—or the minimum number of participants acceptable for a grant. Then look at how much money is made once these basic costs are covered. This is a strategy for seeking more money. "Grantmaker, with the $100,000 you are investing, you are getting 50 persons to this great result. If you wanted to double that total, the added cost is half that amount—$50,000."

4. Cost to milestones. The best projections are done to milestones. "This is what we project spending to get the numbers needed to reach milestone one, then two, etc. It simply apportions money from each line item and places it with each milestone. This gets you away from overspending by category, to overspending by burn rate of money and needed accomplishments at each milestone. I covered this in Chapter 2. It sure helps to cast off the budget as a mindset.

TRY IT

1. Take a stab at costing out an internal activity, such as a recurring meeting, annual staff retreat, or planning cycle, in which you are involved. Project its full cost with staff time defined as all hours that could not be spent on anything else. Get that metric from accounting as needed and make sure it includes payroll taxes and benefits, divided by the days actually worked.

2. Play with costing to milestones. Take a total budget for something and allocate costs to progress points. If there are none, use this chapter to define some generic ones. Then look at how the distribution of money and perhaps even the amount changes.

CHAPTER 14

The Resume: From Qualifications to Achievement Records

While resumes are presumed essential in hiring people, selecting consultants, and choosing conference speakers, they carry a much broader weight. They can speak to the value of people. They are our plumage. A "thin resume" lacks the weight of degrees, position experiences, and publications. An impressive resume is full of experiences, publications, awards, and other honors. The question is whether resumes are an effective way to define achievement. In my view, they are not, especially when most people only look to build their resumes rather than increase the accomplishments they reflect.

Resumes also follow a tight template, reinforced by courses and books on resume writing. Resumes departed from high achievement and are instead used to confirm minimums. "Must have a masters degree and five years of experience." "Let this person through the gate; they are qualified." By this screen, Bill Gates would not have been hired anywhere.

Resumes also reflect an effort to only do things to add them to a resume. High school students are encouraged to do community service. Why? Because it will look good on their resume. Resumes also only portray the right moments. In video resumes, this reaches an extreme. Presentations are tightly edited to make the applicant seem as if they are always happy and smiling while ladling out food at a soup kitchen. In sports, highlight videos catch those very few moments when the resume-holder is a star who makes every basket, hits home runs, or scores touchdowns. Most resumes are intended to promote the ideal you rather than the reality.

Education, Experience, and Upward Mobility

You learn three things from a resume:

1. Level of Education. This carries a presumption of knowledge. You see degrees, professional development programs, and sometimes class ranking. You also see scholarship and assumed thought leadership in articles and books written. What you don't see is the insight needed to shape solutions that fit organizations or the people within them. You also know nothing about learning speed. On the job, a person may take days or just hours to learn and apply something. The status of the specific college, and in some cases high school, are also given weight. This person went to Harvard, Yale, or Stanford. This does predict that they will make higher salaries. It does not predict their energy, motivations, or happiness.

2. Experience. In the listing of previous jobs held, we can see where the person has worked and at what scale. The first problem arises with the simple observation that experience can be good or bad. My daughter found in her School Turnaround program that many of the teachers with 20 years of experience had learned to give up on

kids. Many school superintendents are selected because they have the experience of working in similarly sized districts, even if they were not successful there.

3. Upward mobility. Did the applicant get successive jobs with increased responsibilities? Did they move up organization charts toward top leadership and higher impact? If not, something is off here. It could be either lack of ambition or low performance.

Perhaps neither explanation holds up. Take a person whose resume showed they started as a teacher, then moved up to become an assistant principal, then principal. All fine. What if their next role was a teacher again? Is this slippage? I know two people who had just this resume profile. Both were outstanding teachers and found they had much less impact on students when they rose to administrative positions. They went back to teaching, where they could make a much larger difference.

An early transgression is the "gap year" after high school. Heavens, this person took a year off to go skiing, or to work, or to volunteer before entering college. Thankfully, this practice is now much more accepted for the year after high school, but is often still questioned with gaps later in a career. The premise that all good workers are interested in higher status and pay can prevent recruiters from spotting and keeping talent that thrives on spontaneity.

In Chapter 12, I focused on the activities in a job description. Most resumes close the circle by repeating the tasks and saying they were successfully completed. For example:

* Successfully lead a team of 15 customer service representatives
* Created strategic plan to guide $20 million in new programs

- Had two articles published in peer reviewed journals. Collaborated with external stakeholders, businesses, and agencies to align objectives and goals
- Managed the process of expanding to three new service sites in the last two years

We have little clue what resulted from these completed activities to make them successful. Did the 15 customer service reps make more people happy than under the previous supervisor? Did the 20-million-dollar plan achieve high net gain? Did people read and gain from the publications? Equally important, we do not know the extent to which the applicant was actually the cause of the achievement listed. I once read the resumes of three persons at the same company who were applying for a job at a different organization. All took personal credit for the same achievement.

While resumes often seek a comprehensive look, one popular component goes in the opposite direction. The video seeks to capture people at their best. Here is a person soaring to the basket, reciting Shakespeare brilliantly, or delivering food to the indigenous in another country. These are cherry-picked moments—a country mile away from a good sample of a person's behavior or accomplishments.

From Qualifications to Achievement Records

The resume is a format containing shallow predictive information. In contrast, there are multiple ways to define a person's accomplishments. Here are two:

1. Make it a resume of achievements. This need not be drastic. Just replace each statement of activity with a statement of accomplishment. Here is how that can work for the above four examples of resume activity:
   - In my first year of guiding 15 customer complaint responders, we doubled the number of persons who said

they were highly satisfied with our help and handled an additional 300 complaints without need for additional staff. Further, in previous years, we lost four persons per year due to burnout and job stress. In my first year, we only lost one, and morale rose significantly. Verification is available upon request.

* I managed a strategic plan which led to 50 more people getting and keeping a job. It also developed pipelines to training and employment with six new companies. We also used the plan to increase contributions by 30%—from $72,000 to $96,000. References of those who can tell you how they personally used the strategy to achieve at a higher level are available.

* We focused on a shared commitment to the same results with three other organizations and used that alignment to start a new program in which we all participated. I doubled the number of students reading at grade level within a year—from 28 to 59 students. I have an available verification report, which shows that this change would not reasonably have happened without our working together.

* My nonprofit opened five new sites in the past two years under my leadership. Four of them have at least 20% more participants than was projected. We projected and needed at least 30 new participants from new sites and enrolled 42. Further, we think they are more likely to succeed than entering participants in the past. The predictive factors we created and rely upon are available upon request.

Note that these follow the guidelines for great targets defined in Chapter 1. They include, for example, numbers, not just percentages. I can sound great in saying that I increased contributions by 50%, until you see that they went from $5,000 to $7,500. Note also that the resume reader is given a way to verify accomplishment.

2. Make it a portfolio. Portfolios in art and architecture, and now other fields, are a compilation of a person's best work. Here are my best client solutions, my best writings, and my best programs. Results do the talking rather than degrees and years in the profession. A huge advantage lies in portfolio development. It forces the question of what defines best. Even that is instructure to readers or viewers. Why did the person choose these artifacts to best reflect their capabilities?

I have used this approach with managers, asking them to display their best contributions in thought creation, reports, or performance reviews, and right down to meetings, leadership or participation, and emails. I love to watch people think about the meetings in which they think they added the most value. Another part of a portfolio is responses from others. What is the highest praise a boss or colleagues ever gave to you? This is tough terrain as we are not used to such inquiry.

I worked with a county department in Florida who wanted to put this record in the personnel file of their employees. The leader pointed out that they normally only added something negative to the file. Any write-ups or infractions were to be included. They did not even encourage putting in the good stuff, though there was no prohibition against it. It is fashionable to talk about being asset- or strength-based, but most HR records are of shortfalls and remediation.

Portfolios are one way to show dimensions of achievement not covered by narrowly defined performance. In education, these include stories, poems, and other creative work. By topics and approach, the reader can discern emerging curiosity, divergent thinking, and other dispositions when they are present. What's in your achievement wallet?

Attributes as Predictors of Success

The admissions director at Dartmouth told the story of the first applicant ever admitted almost instantly and with unanimous approval. The recommendation letter that most impressed them came from a janitor. This custodian noted that the applicant was always saying good morning and joining him for a few minutes picking up trash in the hall. The janitor said the student was extraordinarily kind.

I consider three domains that predict a person's likely level of achievement: knowledge, skills, and attributes. Knowledge starts with what you know—including the acronyms of a field and the realm of nonprofits. It then moves to insights and use of information to draw and act on conclusions. It also arrives at the ability to think divergently rather than inside the knowledge box of an advanced degree or position.

Skills are what you know how to do with what you know. They are critically important in technical areas, where a certificate from Google or Microsoft is the part of a resume that matters most. Soft skills, ranging from inspiring staff to promoting and practicing innovation, are equally important. They are lowered in weight, however, because they are deemed hard to measure. They are impossible to measure from a resume, but can be seen by looking at examples. "Name one thing you did that significantly raised morale among those who report to you and, if possible, give us the names of at least three persons whose spirits were raised."

Attributes are different. They speak to who you are and, in my book, are the best predictors of achievement in most human enterprises. Let's see if this holds for you. Think of a teacher you had at a young age who really made a positive difference to you. Have one in mind? How many of you chose that person because they had a master's degree? How many chose a person best explained by 20 years of teaching? Chances are you picked a person who had outsized sparkle and the ability to engage and inspire. Those are attributes, and they are powerful. Imagine an organization with the zest of a school in which all the teachers were as compelling as the one you remember.

Attributes are not seen in the traditional resume. It takes a different kind of format to surface characteristics such as energy, tenacity, and kindness. Rather than hear or listen to a person proclaim these traits, I find assessments can really help. One I have used for years is the Caliper, an instrument I have used for years. It focuses on who a person is as the best way to predict how they will perform. It also has a focus on job fit, understanding that the characteristics needed in one position may not fit another.[29]

My colleagues and I at TRI and Results 1st developed a list of the characteristics most associated with high-achieving staff at all levels of an organization. Here are two examples of traits we include:

Energy. Without it, many projects will begin, but few will finish. And many will begin boldly but end up as weak copies. Positive energy is often the greatest predictor of success. It includes:
- Stamina and staying power
- Enthusiasm and optimism
- Sense of humor

Why is energy so important? First, energetic people get way more done in a day than listless ones. Second, their enthusiasm builds engagement, confidence, and motion in others.

Bias to Act. Many people are—at heart—critics, planners, boosters. Sparkplugs are doers. They want to solve problems, not study or decry them. This includes:

- Focus on solutions
- Sense of urgency
- Opportunity-driven

Why is an itch to act so important? It is the best way to move from a focus on problems to a focus on solutions.

You can see the complete list of characteristics we use and take your own measure of key attributes on our website, results1st.org. Our framework has much in common with others that focus on attributes. One I find compelling is the GRIT framework, developed by Angela Duckworth. From her research, she concludes: "In sum, no matter the domain, the highly successful had a kind of ferocious determination that played out in two ways. First, these exemplars were unusually resilient and hardworking. Second, they knew in a very, very deep way what they wanted. They not only had determination, they had direction."[30]

Can you see and hear attributes in people? Yes! The energetic boss is the one who leaves you with an extra bounce in your stride after you speak with them. The itch to act shows up in how a person spends their time. Both the Achievement Resume and the Portfolio capture who a person is far better than the traditional resume.

1. Create your portfolio. Select the best three examples of your work in the last three years. Make sure you capture achievement in informal settings, not just documents you write. Make a note of what each says about your achievements and who you are as a person.

2. Pick the top three job assignments on your resume—or ones you would list if you were making one. Then add a quick summation of what was accomplished by the organization from the work that you did in each.

CHAPTER 15

The Strategic Plan: From Documents to Designs

Strategic plans are documents that are carefully composed to meet expectations for what they should contain. Few people ask what is to be achieved by having the plan. The document is the result sought by funders, nonprofit rating and information services, and stakeholders. I will often ask an audience how many have been involved in creating a strategic plan. Many raise their hands. I then ask how many were as excited at the fifth meeting of the strategy group as the first. Most hands go down. The first thing we can see is that the development of the strategic plan reduces the energy to do anything differently. The observations and pivot here apply equally to succession, fundraising, and other kinds of plans where the document is the result.

The point should not be to just have a strategic plan. It is to have a strategy. In my experience, the former actually makes the latter much harder to create.

Words at Rest

Strategic plans are stagnant until someone is moved to take action. This also applies to fundraising, succession, sustainability, and other plans. The formats are prescribed, and the process to use them are defined by consultants and traditions. Here are the realities I see time and again:

* You wait to implement anything until the planning process is complete.
* Most people in the organization can't think of one thing they should do differently as a result of having the plan.
* Components of the plan are separately developed then put together by a committee.
* The plan consists of what the planners believe someone else should do differently.
* Widespread agreement is sought as a signal of buy-in. Here is how strategic planning ends:
  Leader: "Thanks so much for all your hard work completing the sections of our plan. We are now gathered to refine the document. Your suggestions?"
* "If we put this section of the plan ahead of that one, it would be a more logical sequence."
* "That paragraph should go to the new spot you note."
* "World class" sounds much better than "excellent."

In wordsmithing the document, have we improved the strategy? No, we have perfected a document.

Planning and acting are not only separate, but sequential. The adage, "First we plan, then we act," is augmented by, "Ready… Aim… Fire." It's actually, "Ready… Aim… Aim some more… Aim some more… Fire." Not much power left by that point, and those with an itch to act have checked out. Further, I rarely see an explicit annual reckoning of what the strategic plan produced last year. Instead, we have the soothing expression of the "rolling plan" for a three-year period. We roll on without pausing to ask what happened with the last plan.

The larger problem is that most plans lack aiming points. Rather, they have goals and objectives, stated on a general level. For example:

* Add and support many more volunteers
* Become a national thought leader in our field
* Diversify our revenue to be less dependent on a few donors
* Enrich the participant experience
* Add summer reading programs

These are activities, not targets. The most discouraging response I hear when I ask what value such general approaches have is that they are inspirational. Since they sound similar to those in the plans of many other nonprofits, it sounds like inspiration comes from fitting in and not standing out.

Where's the Main Course?

One reason strategy is hard to find in a plan is that it is rarely defined. Consider a strategic plan with the usual contents: vision mission, SWOT analysis, pillars, legs, or other structures to indicate key principles or priorities, finances, results and metrics, work plans, financial trends, etc. Strategy is sometimes taken as the amalgam of topics rather than a separable section.[31] All of this leads me to a tongue-in-cheek definition of "strategic:" an impressive adjective to dignify an otherwise listless noun. Priorities are ho-hum. Strategic priorities sound much better. Not to mention strategic retreats, strategic actions, strategic missions—I see it is noon: time for a strategic lunch.

My Results 1st colleagues and I define strategy in a clear and simple way: it is what you need to reach a high target that current approaches cannot achieve. If a group says it will determine its results as a part of strategic planning, it has the order reversed. Strategy is only relevant when you need to do something differently to achieve your goal. If you want a 5% increase in achievement next year, just redouble current efforts. No strategy is needed. Strategy is an intervention into what you or others now do. It is not a soothing confirmation that you are already doing the right things. It also almost invariably involves divergent thinking and innovation. This takes finding people who do that well. Few strategies start with consensus.

A great example comes from Southwest Airlines, which for years was one of the most profitable companies in the US. Its founder, Herb Kelleher, wanted to attract many new customers by making flights cheaper than the bus trip between major Texas cities. This required significantly lower costs and high volume. A 5%, or even 10%, improvement was not enough. Herb created a brilliant strategy and later apologized to an academic gathering that he did not need a plan, a page, a paragraph, or even a complete sentence to state it. Here it is: reduce gate time. At the time, most airline costs were fixed—planes, gates, headquarters functions, etc. Fuel and labor were reasonable. Herb and his cofounder calculated that if they could get two more flights in each day, most of the gross revenue from the last two flights would be net revenue, giving them the money to lower fares.

Let's keep going with Southwest.[32] So how do you reduce gate time? First, you put your strategy in context. Here is an overlay:

* Vision: We see people flying who have never flown before. We see business travelers getting home to say goodnight to their kids. We see employees who want to come to work.
* Results: Be profitable with a 30% decrease in fares.
* Theory of change/logic model: If we have more frequent flights within Texas, more people will fly with

us regardless of cost. If we get the price down 30% or more, we will pull new passengers up to the skies. If we have a sky-high spirit, we will attract the best people.

* Strategy: Reduce gate time.
* Tactics: Clean the plane in the air. Fly only one kind of plane, avoid first class and assigned seats, use only one kind of plane on which pilots and flight attendants are all qualified and familiar.
* Activities: Make the first pass through the cabin right after the last person is served, and speak on PA about people getting into seats quickly. Combine urgency with funny.
* Changes: Listen to everyone who suggests an improved practice, especially to increase customer enjoyment and employee spirit.

Strategy seems like a buried headline until we portray this list differently:

Strategy is the connector between framework and implementation. Ignore it at your peril.

Stopping With the Document

Many strategic plans are completed with the help of consultants, who are often paid by foundations interested in capacity building. Most of the consultants I know have two core skills. First, they know what should go into a plan. They have the format down. Second, they have a process to follow. They know who on staff and board should be involved and when. Both kinds of knowledge assume that the organization knows best, and that their job is to learn the thinking of staff and stakeholders to codify it as a strategic plan. I see this approach as vastly less powerful than charging the consultant to come up with options that have not occurred to the organization. This, however, goes against the grain of the trade, especially in the era of trust philanthropy. Saying that we trust the nonprofit to know the best strategy is questionable. The consultant proudly proclaiming that they start where the client is often means they end there as well.

Most consultants are paid by the product or the hours. When the plan is completed, the consultant's work is done. In my view, the consultant should be paid a small amount for helping develop the plan and a large success fee when the plan is implemented and achieves higher results. My group, Results 1st, loves to play in that sandbox and sets prices based on value rather than time. One of my most frequently reprinted articles discusses Result-Based Consulting with an example of a strategic planning consultant paid less for the plan than for how it works in the first year of using it. A warranty can readily be added.[33]

Consultants are not the only group with no structural connection plan implementation. Most of the planners I see on staff are happy for the plan to consist of what other people should do differently. The only way I know to activate a strategic plan is to identify persons who must do something differently and get their commitment to do so. That belongs in the plan. The plan also needs a way to track progress through the milestone system described in Chapter 2. Plan implementation should be seen as a project.

I like including participants in the plan and commitments to use it. The kinds of community compacts covered in Chapter 7 show far more zest and shared interests than do the responses to plans I see in organizations. Plans as a format contain none of the elements needed to activate them. I do not suggest changing this. Rather, replace plans with two other approaches entirely.

From Plans to Designs

Plans are complete in themselves. Few of us ask what a plan aims to achieve. We ask what's in it. How ironic. I have an alternative approach that comes with an instruction manual and a premise of building something. Designs are different. You design to build something. You build it to achieve something. Results are always in mind. Design thinking is described by Tim Brown in "Change by Design" this way: "The mission of design thinking is to translate observations and insights into products and services that will improve lives." One key is to first identify customer needs then dive into product specification. The point is not to say what the product is, which leads to conventional thinking. Speak to what the product is to achieve. The end of designing is a product. First visualize it, then make it. Try it out on possible customers. These customers could also be your participants, clients, or patients. I like the term customer because they have a choice. They can choose to buy a grill or a program to improve their health or kids' grades. In some cases, I can be mandated to attend, but I cannot be required to change my behavior. Product thinking starts with knowing what people will buy and use. People weigh costs and benefits and consider the elements of the product—from wrapper (first appearance) to warranty (what happens when the product is not working).

I have an example. My group, The Rensselaerville Institute, for years offered self-help programs to build water and wastewater systems in depressed small towns. In our first days, we decided to impress the locals by literally rolling out our display with many steps. It was at least six feet long. This was our wrapper—which we attempted to sell as a process. Residents sat politely as we talked through the process of working together. We had surprisingly few takers. I finally asked a resident of one town, who showed little interest, why we were not connecting. He told me I lost the residents within five minutes. Folks here want stuff they can understand.

We made a big shift based on a question. "How would we sell self-help if we were coming to town to sell kitchen knives or washing machines?" Here was our new presentation:

- What are we selling? We are here to tell you about a product called self-help water line. It means that you do much of the work in return for greatly reduced costs and faster action. We estimate six months.

- What other products might you buy to achieve the same gain? You might just pay for a contractor, although the cost would be very high. You might wait for a government grant, although it looks like that is unavailable given your small size. Or you could buy nothing and hope for the best. The problem is that you will likely run short of water or face a health crisis within the next five years.

- What are the benefits of this product? A water line that will cost no more than $10 per month and a way to bring the community together by putting it in yourselves.

* What are the costs to buy and to use it? The community will have to provide a project sparkplug to lead the project from your end. Each family will need to contribute about 50 hours for not just the line, but handling the paperwork and feeding the volunteer workers. You will also have to deal with handling some persons who may not do their share of the work.

* What are the instructions that come with the product? Let's say it's 6 am one week into the project and the rented backhoe is idling because the four needed workers have not shown up. What do you do about that? Our role would be to either be on site or be on standby every day to handle such problems. We will also have instructions that clearly show tasks such as fitting pipe sections together and helping residents to celebrate at the end of each day for the pipe laid.

* How satisfied are other customers who bought this self-help approach? Here are our reviews. You are encouraged to speak with the people noted.

* Is there a warranty? If you provide all the work hours and worker support needed, we promise to get the money needed to buy the materials and to finance this such that your cost is no more than $20. If we cannot get the loan, we will provide the money ourselves. Please know that we are as dependent on you as you may be on us. If we have just one project bust up in anger or no water, the donors that support us would go away in a hurry.

That approach worked. We went from getting about one in five communities deciding to move forward to four in five. Just as consequential was how we changed what we did. No challenge was stronger than coming up with a warranty. Once we saw how powerful a promise made out of our confidence that the product would work was, we could build it. Many of the programs that nonprofits offer will look different when they are designed rather than planned.

Mapping could be called a different approach. Whether an old-fashioned road map or a digital Google Map, maps begin with the visual distance between where you are now and where you want to go. The first thing I like about maps is that they are hard to wordsmith. People refining their map must find better routes, not better words. The second point is that maps are for motion. I only read a plan, but I use a map. In my view, a map is a tool for design with a strong emphasis on how customers (participants) view things. Maps include these elements:

1. Present location. We are here. To recognize this place, all key descriptors must be shown, including shortfalls in achievement and major challenges. This is a visual prompt to take Tom Peter's admonition to heart to, "Confront the brutal facts."

2. Destination. The metaphor of "life as a journey" is set aside. The trip has a point. It intends to get somewhere specific. It is critical to know when you have arrived. It is also important to make this a far distance from where you are now. If it is easy to reach, just start traveling. Aiming points are literal with any form of geography. You know when you have arrived.

3. Routes. With a paper or digital map, you can select among multiple existing routes. With the route as your strategy, you have to invent the way forward. A number of analogies to road trips apply, including the presence of charging stations that replenish energy.

4. Terrain. What obstacles lie ahead and how will you deal with them? Can you put in a bridge that you could use to get help from another group or resource? Especially if you are hiking or paddling. Are there mountains to climb or streams to cross? Do you envision swamps that might mire you in soft ground?

5. Time. I remember the old AAA Triptiks which showed you a car journey in terms of the sites and the time it will generally take to get from the top of the map section to the bottom. Long-range hikers find this essential for how much water to carry. Maps lend themselves to tracking time by a horizontal axis that notes days, weeks, or hours to know if you are on the pace needed. Digital maps can have an estimated time of arrival.

6. Drivers and passengers. Jim Collins is known for a number of simple principles. One is to get the right people on the bus. The trip to a great result begins with the right team members. It also means that essential people do not bail out, and additional persons can hop aboard when needed.

Maps can work equally well for customers of your designed product, but only if you can use their language. They have their own view of terrain, destination, and routes. I worked with a non-profit in Washington DC to help very disadvantaged clients. The group showed me their written framework constructed with social work language. I asked staff if these words would be understood and used by the people they helped. They said no—their clients would simply say they were stuck. We worked out a way for clients to visualize being stuck as their "present location" and to talk about what it would take to get out of the mud and where they wanted to go once they could move. Drawing and acting are great ways for people to portray where they are and to think about where they want to go.

1. Take a program or an internal function and reframe it as a product which you want to sell to someone. Include gains, costs, appearance, instructions. And if you had to offer a warranty, what would it say?

2. Start a map. Begin with present location–the top three points of accomplishments and top three shortfalls in present success. Then locate your destination across the page or screen with the top three specific achievements that will reflect your arrival there. Then start playing with lines that reflect different approaches to get from present to defined future.

CHAPTER 16

The Logic Model: From Theory to Informed Actions

Models can be a highly disciplined way of showing effects from the interactions of many factors in a given field. Hurricane modeling warns governments and residents where and when to take action. Economic models are designed to predict what will happen with specified shifts in monetary policy, consumer behavior, and many other factors. Models get better based on performance. Meteorologists choose the weather models to rely upon for the next storm based on the models that proved most accurate in the last one.

The logic models, theories of change, and similar formats in the nonprofit world are very different. They are not portraying disciplined relationships and are rarely put to any test of prediction. The models I see are primarily formatted as lists grouped into categories. Where the funder requires a logic model, the nonprofit goes to training to make sure they have the right words in the right column.

Logic by Columns

I have reviewed hundreds of logic models and find little variation, not just in format, but in content. Here is one very typical set of columns and listings within them.[34]

Such lists appear equally in high- and low-performing group logic models. Note that there is nothing said about what has to be in an input to make it of value. These are treated as commodities. No particular requirements for great staff or partners are included.

The next column, Output, is where many formats have several categories. Here is an example:

INPUTS	OUTPUTS	
	Activities	Participation
What We Invest	**What We Do**	**Who We Reach**
Staff	CONDUCT:	Participants
Volunteers	workshops	
Time	meetings	Clients
Money	DELIVER:	Agencies
Research	services	
Base		Decision-makers
Materials	DEVELOP:	Customers
Equipment	products	
Technology	curriculum	Satisfaction
Partners	resources	
	TRAIN	
	PROVIDE:	
	counseling	
	ASSESS	
	FACILITATE	
	PARTNER	
	WORK WITH MEDIA	

Sounds logical. We conduct workshops and reach participants and clients. We have no idea what "reaching" means, and "work with media" tells us nothing about what should result from doing so.

The third column focuses on outcomes or impacts.

OUTCOMES – IMPACT		
Short-Term	**Medium-Term**	**Long-Term**
What the short-term results are	**What the medium-term results are**	**What the ultimate impact(s) is**
Learning	**Action**	**Conditions**
Awareness	*Behavior*	*Social*
Knowledge	*Practice*	*Economic*
Attitudes	*Decision-making*	*Civic*
Skills	*Policies*	*Environmental*
Opinions	*Social Action*	
Aspirations		
Motivations		

Does this mean that attitude change should always precede behavior change? Many programs see a reverse sequence. In some cases, motivations take shape once practice change begins. Note, also, the blending of words. The column is called outcomes, and the lists speak of results and impacts. Nothing is offered to differentiate these terms. Also, we have no idea whether short-term means a week or a year.

Now, let's zoom out to see the logic that connects inputs, outputs, and outcomes. It's—arrows!

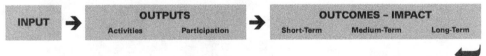

This ubiquitous sign of progression is so easy to add to a graphic. If only the arrow made that happen. Note, also, how the arrow reverses at the end to show a tidy closed loop. The model turns full circle.

Another approach to creating logic is called Theory of Change. I find it very similar. The below is a typical description by a group supporting the approach:

A theory of change describes the logical sequence of steps expected to lead to a desired outcome or impact. It is a way of thinking about and planning for change. It helps organizations clarify their goals and strategies, identify the resources and interventions needed to achieve them, and measure progress over time.

This group goes on to list four critical steps:

* First, please define the problem or challenge: Clearly explain the problem or challenge the organization is trying to address.

* Identify the desired outcome or impact: Define the long-term, transformative change that the organization aims to achieve.

* Map out the logic of change: Identify the intermediate outcomes or outputs needed to reach the desired impact. These outcomes or outputs should be specific, measurable, and achievable.

* Identify the key activities or interventions: Identify the specific activities or interventions implemented to achieve the intermediate outcomes or outputs.

As with logic models, the focus is on highly generalized activities. How many times do we read, "Listen to and act with community," and, "Build equity, leadership, and accountability." When I ask nonprofit staff to tell me the logic or theory that connects what they do to what they achieve, I am often told that this is contained in their logic model. They want to pull it up before answering. How can logic be helpful when staff do not know what it is?

From Models to Informed Actions

We do want logic for a program that connects what you do to what you achieve. To make that happen, however, I find it helpful to think of the model or theory as a prompt for action. Its value is to establish guidelines that help staff decide what to do next. In the Southwest example:

* "Why am I making the first pass through the plane soon after all passengers are served?"
* "Because this cues people not to toss stuff on the floor."
* "Why is this important?"
* "By cleaning the plane in the air, the airline avoids a clearing crew at the gate, which would slow turn-around."

The best models and theories for nonprofits help everyone—including participants—make their behavior intentional to success.

One way to pivot is to start with your logic model and add a result-based subheading for each entry. Start with inputs and note what each must include to be counted as useful. For the logic model listed above, for example:

Volunteers—We need at least 15 volunteers who show great ability to engage our participants and be present at least twice a week for an hour.

Partners—We need a group that will co-own our results and is highly successful in getting kids to grade-level reading. We need a second effective group which provides mentors with whom our participants want to hang out.

These kinds of statements take generic inputs and tailor them to what you need. For outputs, make it clear just what they must produce. For example:

—Deliver prevention services. The programs must engage participants so that at least 75% can say that they have changed their behavior to reduce the likelihood of the problem occurring.

—Provide alcohol-free alternatives for youth. At least 25% of youth who have a choice of great alcohol-free drinks actually choose to drink them.

For Outcomes—Impact, drop the short-, medium-, and long-term subcategories as artificial distinctions. Learning, for example, does not always come first. Sometimes, action is the prompt for learning. Instead, put in a subheading of "Intended Results" and list your targets. Then add a subheading of broader impacts and list the likely additional gains that will come from hitting a target. The point is not to leave your intentions and commitments in the model or theory. The logic must be tightly connected to what you want to achieve and what it takes in inputs and outputs to get there.

If... Then

Even with consequences added, the traditional logic model says little about how inputs prompt outputs and outputs lead to results. I like getting to that in a different way. Think of your logic as a set of IF... THEN assumptions. If we do this, then that will happen. This simple approach puts your logic where you want it to be: offering predictions. Doing this predicts that. This is the only way to make your behavior intentional.

One way to do this is to ask each output what has to be included to predict achievement. Just make a list of the 5 to 20 If... Then assumptions that most guide your program. One critical guideline: make the "Then" about results. One reason I am not a fan of the input-output progression is that it is both too easy and too weak. The question needs to be what has to be included in your curriculum, counseling, or other service that directly forecasts success.

Here are some examples of If... Then statements I have used to help scores of nonprofits. I suggest you not start by fitting these into a traditional logic model.

* If we ask participants to define intended gains in their own terms, then they will achieve more than if we were to use professional language.

* If everyone in our organization can say one way in which what they can do will directly increase participant gain, we will achieve far more than if only the persons with defined roles in a project do so.

* If we only get half the number of participants we envisioned, but they are all deeply and personally committed to success, we will end with a higher result than we would with casual commitment from a much larger number.

* If we have a clear idea of which persons are at risk for dropping out or falling short at an early point, we can do far more to help them achieve than if we only learn this at or near program end.

* If someone starts to apply what they learned in the first three days after each session ends, the chances meteorically rise that they will get gains from the program.

* If the participant believes that what they do makes a difference, they are far more likely to take action to apply what they learned.

If you prefer a simpler and more declarative approach, just use statements that are clear and critical. One of my favorites: Information is seldom enough to change behavior. You work with participants or audiences to form and apply convictions that change what they do.

Now comes another and equally potent approach. Ask everyone in the program to name one thing they do that is not prescribed but makes a real difference for participants or their internal customers. My daughter, while principal of an elementary school in New York City, reflects an example. She concluded that if she could know and use the names of over half of her 800 students while greeting them each morning in the hall, it would make her a positive and active force on the shop floor of the school. Nowhere is this listed in the logic model of a school, which is not a prompt for day-to-day action.

TRY IT

1. List three "If… Then" assumptions that express the logic that connects what you do to what you achieve. Then get a conversation going with at least one colleague on how well these assumptions have held up in completed projects.

2. Define what you can do to best use the assumptions and express the logic connecting activity with its consequences. Think of this as your personal logic model!

CHAPTER 17

The Proposal: From Request to Investment Opportunity

If the sole consequence of writing proposals was getting money, I would not include this format as a major influencer of nonprofit work. The mindset and practice of proposals, however, does not stop with the pitch for funds. It influences many forms of internal work and external communications. As with other formats, the content includes very little about the targets an organization sets and the degree to which they reach them.

Write Your Way In

Nonprofits have a curious expression to describe what they do to get money. They "write a grant." The Foundation Center (now combined with Guidestar as Candid) has for years offered courses on effective proposal writing, and its books and materials remain widely used. There are well over 50 books. They include: "The Complete Book of Grant Writing," "Learn To Write Grants Like a Professional," and "Grant Writing for Dummies." The focus is on creative writing. The problem is that the project for which you are seeking funds is not supposed to be fiction.

I do not blame nonprofits for seeing proposal creation as an art form. While at TRI, I needed to raise about $4 million each year to support our programs. We endured the realities of overlapping words and the ambiguity of what it meant when the funder said that a given area was a priority. What we learned was to be responsive. Whatever the funder wanted, we tried hard to provide. This focus continued through reports, site visits, news coverage, and every other aspect of our relationship.

Almost everything in a result frame should hinge on effective forecasting. The question here is whether the great proposal predicts the great project to follow. Some years ago, I worked with two foundations on this question. They each selected 25 projects where they knew two things: 1) The grade they had given the project (great, sufficient, barely acceptable) and 2) The grade they would give the projects' results. When they compared grades, they found a very small correlation. Here are some proposal features that help to explain why the proposal is such a thin read for funding programs:

* Focus is on the problem. The needs statement is often given considerable weight with the assumption that understanding a problem is the key to solving it. Is it? The correlation between a fine needs statement and a great project to follow is actually weak. A stronger correlation is with the presence of a grants writer who can efficiently secure and present data from the internet. Also note that there is no comparable weight put on opportunities. We go deep with plight and shallow with solutions.

* Results are a piece, not the point. Especially in government grant programs, points are spread across many

factors, and high totals for other sections can be high enough to overcome a low score on intended accomplishment. Further, the sections leading to points are considered to be separate. The document portraying the project is linear, and results are a piece, not the point.

* Emphasis is on what the group will do. Project descriptions encourage a narrative on the activities nonprofits and their participants will undertake. This often takes the form of a workplan or timeline to which elements are fitted. Where accomplishments enter in the form of "deliverables" in a scope of services. Short shift is given to the critical element of who brings the approach alive with participants.

* The document has just one use: to get money. When I ask nonprofits what value the proposal has once it is approved, most say it is only consulted to be reminded of reporting and other requirements. The nonprofit needs two documents. One is to get the money. The other is to spend it.

A broader challenge is that the proposal format structure separates nonprofit staff who get the money from those who spend it. When I ask project directors what they are on the hook for achieving, many cannot tell me without looking it up in the proposal or grant agreement. More importantly, the grants writer is off to tackle their next proposal. They are not encouraged to play any role that ties promise to reality. They should stick around. They are the nonprofit's stewards of results.

From Proposals to Investment Requests

Proposals are pitches that are given to funders of programs. An increasing number of foundations have shifted to see themselves as in the business of investing in results. Their core-know changes from distributing money to getting the most possible gain for the dollars they have available. Most foundations and individual donors lie between these endpoints. One general tendency for all but the most traditional grant makers is to stop favoring a long length of proposals. Not only does this take much more time to read and process, but the long document is gradually understood to obfuscate more than clarify. This prompts my first advice: shorten your writing to directly respond to the questions or topics. You are likely to be praised—especially by the grant reviewer who picked up your document, likely the eighth one read that day. While you cannot change the proposal format, you can change how you use it.

In some cases, you can use your own format within general guidelines. My first advice is to resist inserting the same categories and long-winded responses that other grant makers require. Rather than expounding on the need, for example, why not consider saying:

We will not burden you with an extended needs analysis for two reasons. First, you already know about the problem and how many have it. Second, our focus is on solving the problem, not showing you how we can use secondary sources to describe it. Our needs statement will focus on responding to two questions:

1) What has happened over the last five years regarding the nature of this need and the number who have it in our geography?

2) What is known about niches or segments in the overall need that require different responses?

Nonprofits have great flexibility in their own fundraising materials, of course. The best example is the case book. This can truly be an investor request. Here you need not follow the standard format of a brochure or other information document. To avoid that, you begin with what the interested donor wants to know. That comes next.

Answering Investor Questions

Investors in results do not want to read a proposal filled with narrative statements. They want data points relevant to three questions:

* What are we buying? When our money is gone, just what will be different and for whom will it be different?
* What are the chances those results will happen? Do the group and project hit the factors that we see as the best predictors of project success?
* Is this the best way to spend our money? Does it offer the greatest gain possible for the dollars we have available?

Where you can do so, I suggest you package your pitch as investment requests. This is the gain to which we are committed. This is why it will happen. Here is evidence that shows it is the best possible investment you can make. Let's look at each question.

With what the investor is getting, you pull in results with the characteristics defined in Chapter 1. If you have clear results, you can almost always state them in a paragraph. You can also add broader and deeper impact from achieving the result. Most health, education, and social service achievements have a gain in at least two areas. The social determinants of health, for example, intertwine with the social determinants of educational achievement. In other cases, the impact is how deep the gain goes. In some cases, it is life-changing.

I also favor specifying value from gains. Start with economics. For each at-risk student who graduates high school thanks to a program, data suggest the gain in lifetime income is over $500,000, and the reduced draw on government funds is generally equivalent to that. You do want to be specific and avoid vague estimates such as many multiplier effects. Saying that your event brought in $2 million to the community may not be supportable. And if the gain was earned by highly profitable restaurants and vendors, what value is that to the investor in human gain?

When determining what the chances are that the result will happen, note that the proposer knows the key predictors and has them covered. I often ask both foundation and nonprofit staff what they see as the key predictors of a great project for which support is needed. Most speak to organizational factors like leadership, sustainability, reputation, and financial management. I have a different list and have guided many foundations in using it:

- Past success. The best predictor of achievement is not what you say you will achieve next year. It is what you actually achieved last year.
- Highly effective people. Your project leadership and delivery persons matter as much or more than program design. Degrees and experience do not predict success.
- Strategy known to work. Do you have a way to make work intentional to results, to have comparative advantage, or to exclude some current activities?
- Verification framework embedded in the program that tells staff and participants where they need to change to be successful.
- Clear milestones that show flow of participants through critical success points.
- Steep learning curve. Change happens at the speed of seeing shortfalls and changing things.

The first two factors, in my experience, are the most predictive. One group gives you lofty vision and very impressive targets. Another tells you how much they achieved in the last three years. Which is more impressive? A group unable to say anything on results with the last grant they received is not likely to be seen as a great investment. Individual staff are equally critical. For many participants, they *are* the program.

Next you will want to express why your group is the best bet for support. Most nonprofits know little about other groups in the same space and are justifiably reluctant to position themselves at the expense of others with whom they work. They leave it to the investor to select among applicants. This is often a bad idea, since most foundations lack good ways to do this and may rely on familiarity. Your response need not involve negative statements about other groups. You just need data points that show your specific level of achievement on specific yardsticks. One is cost per gain, as covered in Chapter 9. Even if you cannot be precise, it tells the investor you are focused on their return on charitable money. While you cannot speak to this metric for other groups, you can find data at the state and national level that at least nudge toward comparative analysis.

Three other factors I think of as value-adding. If groups are close in appeal, these can make the difference. One is how tightly their results are verified. An increasingly seen limitation of the national rating and information services, such as Guidestar and Charity Navigator, is that they rely on self-reported data. Anything that verifies achievement from an independent perspective is very helpful. The second is whom you serve and where you live. If you have strong results for persons, cultures, or neighborhoods where no one else is effectively helping, say so. Scalability is a third value added. Many foundations give this weight, although some speak of scaling programs before they know how successful they are. Chapter 10 looks at scaling approaches as needed to move needles.

Enter the Prospectus

While I am not inclined to praise corporate practice as the key to nonprofit effectiveness, enterprise does offer a format that offers far richer data to prospective investors than does the proposal. The prospectus is the document used to attract investment capital, often for start-ups or the significant expansion of an existing business. It is typically printed on thin paper with no color. The warmth and opportunity does not come from smiley faces. It comes from data. Here are five features of the prospectus and how nonprofits could use that discipline in program proposals, annual appeals, capital campaigns, and other fundraising. I use language from an actual prospectus to illustrate each point.[35]

1. The latest information. "We have not, and the underwriters have not, authorized anyone to provide any information or to make any representations other than those contained in this prospectus…" In contrast, nonprofit donors are unsure if the latest information is on the website, in a brochure, a proposal, a report, or on a website like Charity Navigator or GuideStar.

2. Disciplined use of language. "Certain Terms Used in this Prospectus." This section of the prospectus carefully defines key terms. In contrast, the proposal format allows for such terms as results, outcomes, and impacts to be used interchangeably.

3. Risk factors. "Our future success depends on our ability to successfully adapt our business strategy to changing home-buying patterns and trends." In contrast, fundraising appeals suggest that if you give us the money, great things will assuredly happen. Any group that does not identify risks has no easy way of dealing with them when they occur. Also, they cannot make the case that high return may need a lower probability of success.

4. Past results. "We increased our revenues from $490.9 million for the nine months ended September 30, 2019,

to $672.7 million for the nine months ended September 30, 2020." When was the last time you read in a fundraising appeal headline what they achieved for those served last year. To the nonprofit, this is history. To enterprise, it is likely the future.

5. Use of proceeds. "The monies generated are considered sufficient for the following purposes." Unlike budgets in a proposal, the prospectus must make rational the amount of money requested relative to the gains stated.

Results 1st has a product called Result Money. It has guidelines and many examples of how to get more money based on your achievement. See it on our website.

TRY IT

1. Make a list of the top five factors that you and a colleague see as critical in predicting success. Look at actual experience, not the categories in proposals or operational plans. Then ask what you should do to make sure each is fully covered.

2. Outline the content for a prospectus seeking investment in an area where you write proposals. Use the categories in this chapter and see what difference this makes in what you say. If possible, use it with a result-focused contributor to get their take.

PART III NOTES

27. The fluid use of words in change projects is unhelpful and often glib. In the Newark schools project described in Chapter 10, Dale Rusakoff in her study says this: "They divided strategies into 'buckets' such as the accountability bucket, the teacher-evaluation bucket. They took liberties with parts of speech, changing nouns into verbs—as in, Bucket those two ideas together—and adverbs into nouns, as when Anderson referred to her expertise in 'behindedness,' or students who were several years behind their grade level." Words flow forward and upward so much faster than deeds!

28. In an ideal world, the org chart and the culture of an organization would align. If a group says that its culture is to empower all staff to make decisions and has five layers between the top and the bottom, how can this work? The CDC head quote is telling: culture and org chart are mutually distinct. They serve different purposes. My view is that results are the best convening point.

29. One example of attributes needing to fit a role is the difference in traits needed to build a new enterprise and manage it once fully formed. A start-up needs a person with high energy and stamina, abundant confidence, and the ability to persuade others to join a venture not yet proven. An established organization needs details, systems, and at least some uniformity. I like books like "Strength Finders" for their consideration of many dispositions. The alignment with role, however, is always important to know which ones most matter.

30. "Grit" is the product of Angela Duckworth, who combines academic and consulting viewpoints. The book has sold over one million copies and with good reason. It offers more evidence than do such inventories on how its traits correlate with success. Check out the ten-item Grit Scale—on page 55 of the hardbound Scribner edition from 2018. Find your own grit quotient, a metric that applies to most, if not all job success.

31. I once asked a senior person at a large bank to name the strategy his organization was now using. He wanted to get the words right and picked up the strategic plan. I watched him scan the contents page for the chapter entitled strategy. There was none. Look at your strategic plan. Where is your strategy

stated clearly, and do you differentiate it from vision and logic above and tactics and activity below?

32. If you want a visual look at the early years of Southwest, see "Herb and His Airline," an insightful 60 Minutes segment from years ago. CEO Kelleher's flamboyance shone through, as did his shrewdness. I showed this to nonprofit and government groups in a program I led called Managing New York and asked if they could see any application of Herb's approach to their organization. Almost half said yes. While they could not be that inventive, they felt they could have a strategy that everyone in the organization could express.

33. I have long had a warranty. If you are not entirely pleased with the value of my help in achieving something, you can dock my pay by any amount you choose. My daughter used one in her School Turnaround program. If a school does not hit its agreed upon target (typically for number of students reading at grade level), the program will either refund the money or stay another year without cost. Which would you rather have: a wonderful statement of a consultant's beliefs and values, or a warranty? "Result-based consulting" is included in the Results 1st website section for book readers.

34. The logic model included is from the Division of Cooperative Extension at the University of Wisconsin. I could have picked a hundred other ones. I cringe at how readily specific models fill in the name while changing little in the logic. The logic, apparently, is universal. Divergent thoughts have little place in most time-honored formats, including this one.

35. The prospectus cited was offered by a home-building group seeking $124 million. Similar content areas are in all such documents. While the analogy is not perfect, I like the way it defines information sought by investors who have many options from which to choose. The fits seems strong with a case book where definition of return on grants and contributions can and must be stated crisply.

PART IV

New Directions in
Where the Money Goes

*Every moment is an organizing opportunity,
every person a potential activist, every minute a
chance to save the world.*

— Delores Huertas

*If one really wishes to know how justice is ad-
ministered in a country, one does not question the
policemen, the lawyers, the judges, or the protected members of the middle class. One goes to the
unprotected—those, precisely, who need the law's
protection most!—and listens to their testimony.*

— James Baldwin

Philanthropy in general and foundations in particular have seen
two major shifts in where their money goes. One is the greatly increased focus on collective solutions to solve big problems.
The premise is that we cannot move needles in a given geography
by continuing to work as separate and uncoordinated nonprofits,

governments, civic groups, and philanthropists. The second is the focus on diversity, equity, and inclusion (DEI). The premise is that without more explicit attention to inequities, the appalling gaps in money, attention, and achievement among races, genders, and other factors will continue. Diversity and equity are now the leading topic of national and state associations of grant makers.

I am a strong believer in both directions and devote a chapter to each. My first quest is to show that both can gain accomplishment by a stronger and clearer difference on the results they seek. The question for both collective impact and DEI is not who is at the table, but what they do and achieve once they are there.

CHAPTER 18

Partnerships, Coalitions, Initiatives, Collaborations

Some foundations now spend over half their grant monies on large initiatives that are to bring together many groups to solve problems. The usual focus is on a specific metropolitan area—often a large one. These initiatives tend to seek inclusiveness and diversity as well as widespread agreement among actors.

Variations on a Theme

Partnerships, networks, coalitions, partnerships, networks, and collaboratives—the names are largely interchangeable. As long as groups are working together, we have collective action. In 2011, the Stanford Social Innovation Review published an influential article called "Collective Impact." It advanced the idea that shared work and resources could solve a broad range of economic, environmental, and social problems. From the website of the Collective Impact Forum comes this definition:

"Collective impact is a network of community members,

organizations, and institutions who advance equity by learning together [and] aligning and integrating their actions to achieve population- and systems-level change."

The words stay uplifting but very general as the description continues:

"Social Current activates the power of the social sector by bringing together a dynamic network of human/social service organizations and partners. Leveraging the collective experience of the field and research, we energize and activate the sector and drive continuous evolution and improvement. Together with our network, Social Current amplifies the work of the social sector through collaboration, innovation, policy, and practice excellence."

In general, collective action is a coordination function, not a change mechanism. It pulls together existing approaches to work in a more aligned way that does not challenge what they do. Thus we have terms like, "fostering reinforcing activities," "leveraging the collective experience," and "having a team dedicated to aligning and coordinating the work of the group." The logic and theory of change seems to be that we will get much more done together than we do separately and no one needs to change what they do now beyond increased cooperation.

The Record to Date

If we look at collective action in terms of return on investment, the record is far from sterling. The first reason is cost. The more cost rises, more gain is needed to justify it. The primary use of money is time. Here is an example of the costs of togetherness:

* Two leaders spend a year setting up, coordinating, raising money, handling disagreements, writing reports (3,000 hours).

- Eight members of the steering committee meet monthly for two hours (288 hours).
- Twenty-five nonprofit coordinators spend 20 hours a month furthering the collective agenda (6,000 hours).
- Fifty nonprofits and stakeholders convene quarterly (600 hours).

This comes to 9,888 hours. If we take an average cost per hour (netted for sickness and vacation and with share of overhead) of $60, the tab is $593,280. These are costs just for initiative administration. They include no hours spent helping people to higher achievement.

But Hal, we have to pay people anyway, so there is no real cost. My response is that if there is nothing else these persons might be doing to add value, why are they there?

Let's now turn to gains and look at the challenges of strong, on-the-ground results from collective action. Key factors are nicely detailed in two program evaluations which looked squarely at major shortfalls in achievement. Both were published by foundations who wanted to understand why results for persons in need fell far short of expectations. Both are succinct and very insightful. "Hard Lessons about Philanthropy and Community Change from the Neighborhood Improvement Initiative (NII)" focused on learnings from a William and Flora Hewlett Foundation initiative to improve the lives of residents in three California Bay Area communities.[36] The program ran from 1996 to 2006 and started with $20 million. One conclusion:

"Despite the huge investment of financial and human resources, however, the NII fell far short of achieving the hoped-for tangible improvements in residents' lives. While some stakeholders view characterizing the NII as a failure as too harsh, it certainly was a great disappointment."

The second report, called Midcourse Corrections to a Major Initiative, is a report commissioned by the James Irvine Foundation at the midpoint of an initiative to improve educational performance of students in five localities in California who were low-achieving. The program was called Communities Organizing Resources to Advance Learning (CORAL).[37] It was defined for eight years, ending in 2007, and had $60 million allocated. Here's a summary of the CORAL experience from this report:

> "But the CORAL initiative had all of these elements: smart, capable staff, and regular executive and Board reviews. Yet, at its midpoint—four years and over $40 million invested—it was experiencing serious implementation problems. The number of participants fell far short of the agreed-upon goals. Cost per participant was more than double that which could be supported by public funding streams. The observed quality of the programming was poor to moderate. Programming aimed specifically at the initiative's fundamental goal—increasing educational per—was either weak or nonexistent."

Both reports are insightful, clear, and blunt. You might ask whether these findings are outdated or now irrelevant. Sadly, no. In 2022, I was asked to comment on six major foundation-driven initiatives and found that all were falling short of intentions. When I looked deeper, I saw the same reasons surfacing over and over. These are essential to understand if we are to reach the potential of creating and implementing stronger solutions.

1. Results play little role in design and implementation. The Hewett-Foundation's NII program began with six goals:
   - Connect fragmented efforts to address poverty-related issues in select communities.
   - Improve the capacity (proficiency and resources) of participating community-based organizations.

- Improve Bay Area community foundations' capacity to support neighborhood improvement.
- Develop neighborhood leaders by creating a vehicle for increasing resident involvement in neighborhood planning and improvement strategies.
- Leverage significant public/private resources to support community improvement.
- Provide long-term statistical evidence of changes in poverty indicators (eg, unemployment, welfare dependency, vacant and abandoned structures).

These are all activities. They speak to what the helpers will do, not what those in need will get or do with what they have learned.

2. Structure and process define the program. Steering committees, meetings, policies, and visions, along with timelines and roles, are produced. Processes such as building trust and working to robust agreement if there is no consensus are enacted. In many cases, this can take six months to a year. Similar shared protocol lies in the criteria for suggesting groups and key persons to play a role. They are those who: a) have programs in the geography defined and/or b) are considered influential players. There is almost never a strong effort to differentiate among nonprofits and stakeholders on the basis of previous achievement.

A broader challenge is the assumption in most collective actions that we do it together. This invariably sands off sharp edges of divergent thoughts, which might bring just two or three groups together. Most team players are sensitive to maintaining the smooth waters of agreement. Indeed, in a few cases, the interpersonal connections among those in the action are very strong. The collective can have admirable cohesion. Almost never does it extend, however, to more than a few persons in the community receiving help.

3. Critical assumptions do not hold up. Almost all initiatives I have seen assume something that must come true. In the NII report, that assumption was that after-school programs have a strong influence on academic achievement. The NII report included this finding after early results fell short:

   - It is very difficult to change educational performance through after-school programming. Some scholars said that, given the modest hours involved compared to in-school time, it is nearly impossible.

   - It is likely especially difficult to change educational performance without direct connections to the skills or knowledge tested by schools.

   - Those students with the poorest school performance and greatest need for help are likely to lack basic literacy skills, rendering approaches like homework help largely ineffective.

   The stronger assumption is that after-school programs must have a strong connection with the classroom teacher and instruction to be highly effective. Assumptions should not be set aside lightly. I see this happening with individual enrichment programs where the nonprofit says that its students come from many different schools and that it is impossible to build relationships with all of their teachers. An assumption is not made less useful by being hard to follow.

Time needed is another assumption that often breaks down. Things always take longer than assumed, especially when so many moving parts and viewpoints in collective action must be balanced. From the COR-AL evaluation:

"In Pasadena's first year of work, the challenges of widespread community organizing, nonprofit collaboration, school involvement, and program creation emerged. Progress was slower than planned or hoped for. Getting key players in the community to meet, agree on an educational agenda, and establish roles for working together on an after-school program—all of these activities prove staff- and time-consuming."

4. The connection between those who live in a setting and those there to help is not clear. While foundations and nonprofits talk about theory of change, what is often more critical and seldom addressed is their theory of intervention. The eminent social critic Lewis Mumford pointed out to me that this was a fatal flaw in major anti-poverty programs in the 1960s such as Model Cities. As he put it, the problem was a lack of any theory of intervention. How does outside money and know-how get into a setting? Mumford thought that money was a poor starting point. He favored structural interdependence. I asked him what that meant. It means, he said, that you can't readily leave town if your advice turns sour.

We followed his insights and arranged to buy Stump Creek, PA, from a landlord who bought it from the coal company when the vein played out. We did so with a bank loan. They knew about loan default and that we could not leave any more than they could.

In the James Irvine report, power and prerogative issues came to the fore and stayed that way:

"And in all sites, angst over how the outcomes framework was introduced overwhelmed the discussion about what outcomes should frame the work."

If there is a universal adage in community development, it would be, "Involve the residents." We tend to limit engagement to their suggestions. Put differently, we can understand their situation and their pain, but we fail to understand them as instruments of solution.

5. Energy wanes and sparkplugs leave. When I am at achievement from collaborative work, I always ask participants to tell me what has happened to their level of enthusiasm during the collective action project. Almost no one told me they were more energized at the 5th or 10th meeting of the collaborative than the first. The pattern is well known and seen. Leaders come to meetings for the first month or two when excitement is high. Then they send a staff member who is to represent them. Then we go down the bench until substitutes who have no choice are found. This is a symbol of gradually eroding personal investment. It becomes lethal when it gets to the ground and discourages those with an itch to act.

As with individual nonprofits, movements are explained by their movers and shakers. In her insightful book, "Within Our Reach," Lizbeth Shore set out to define key approaches that worked in critical social problem areas. Early in the book, it was clear she was captivated by a handful of very impressive people.[38]

Collaborations vs. The Other C Words

Many of the words we used to describe how to bring together and sustain a diverse set of nonprofits and other players begin with C. We have communication, coordination, and cooperation. These words assume essential differences and look for a way to keep the groups in sync. A forth C word is or could be very different: collaboration. Collaboration seeks new solutions by which the collaborators achieve far more than the sum of their individual accomplishments. Collaboration is an act of creation, not of agreement. Peter Schrage has a great definition and many examples of how it works in his classic book "Shared Minds."[39] He looks at effective collaborations over many fields. From his and other research with similar findings, I have generated my top five elements of successful collaborations:

1. Small numbers. Collaborations are often duos or trios. The interactions are concentrated and personal. They often rely on very high, but very distinct capabilities— such as partners who create Broadway musicals: one person specializes in the story, the other the music. I have seen heads of nonprofits do this as well, meeting as individuals to shape a joint program or merger. Sure, they had to sell and refine it with staff, but it began with two leaders musing.

2. Off-script inquiry. In contrast to the defined steps in planning, collaboration at its best is improvisation and can get personal and intense. When Francis Crick won the Nobel prize for the double helix discovery, he said that, "Politeness is the poison of all good collaboration in science." Improvisation means sparks that illuminate. Collaborations make up the few rules they need as they go along.

3. Clarity on success. Collaborations have a clear end in sight. This could be a scientific discovery, a broadway musical, or a new way to accelerate getting more homeless persons into transitional homes. Most collaborators have a higher need for achievement than for control or being well-liked. If they see something useful, it does not have to come from them. They start with the result of creating something useful.

4. Time-compressed. Most collaborations have a sense of urgency. Collaborators can be impatient and tend to perch on the wings of opportunities more than on the sturdy framework of problems. These persons thrive on energy, which almost always increases with acceleration and is almost always depressed by slowing down. There will be a time for deliberation and voiced cautions—just not yet. They may have a calendar deadline, but most do not need one.

5. Built for use. Collaborations are not inventions. They are about applying something that brings value to those who use it. Most collaborations have customers and, during or immediately after a solution is clear, the creation is tested. Either audiences like the play or not. Either other nonprofits use your creation of a code-approved tiny house or they do not. Steve Jobs, the legendary head of Apple, once said that people don't know what they want until you show it to them.[40]

Can collective action be collaboration? Probably not, but it can house collaborations. Collective action can work for very small groups who:

* Put results first. "We are gathering a small group of nonprofits that wants, within three years, to cut in half

the number of students not at grade level in reading. Are you in?"

* Encourage variation within the umbrella. "Who's got an idea for a new approach and a partner to try it with? We will grubstake you."

* Is there a leader of your efforts to collect and distribute best practices, benchmarking, and other forms of learning. "We have identified three collective actions spread across the city which have outstanding results. Who really wants to learn how they did it and achieve likewise?"

* Bring in residents. "Three residents and two staff have gathered to define results and set targets for this collective action. The rest of us will listen in. Who will volunteer to show us how this might go?"

Collective Action Turnaround

We have focused on new collective actions. What about the hundreds of existing networks and partnerships growing stale after a year or more? Given how much time and money went into creating and sustaining them to date, can we use them as the foundation for a turnaround? I think so. Here's an example:

My client was a community foundation in North Carolina. It had for years supported a collaborative effort to increase health gains. I was brought in when the foundation began to see a real fall-off from the monthly meetings. I called some of the participants and was told that the meetings had gone stale and nothing happened as a result of talking.

I guided the next meeting, which focused on the problem low-income folks not getting care during pregnancy. I suggested we quickly set a target. It took a while, as some kept asking for a baseline and more information. I noted that any ambitious target would do. The group agreed that getting 40 more individuals prenatal care would be a good target.

I then asked if anyone present could think of a way to get at least a few of those 40 people seen by a doctor in the next two weeks. A participant said he knew the leader of an OBGYN practice and thought they would agree to see two to four patients who were lacking prenatal care pro bono. "Great," I said. "How about calling them now. Just step to the back of the room and see if they will help. Ask if they would mind if we shared their generosity with those assembled." The call was made, and within 10 minutes, we had 10% of our target in hand.

Turnarounds in business are not gradual, gentle changes. They are interventions like my different starting point in North Carolina. They almost always require new leadership. Gillian Williams had a principle about principals in School Turnaround: if a person had led a failing school for three or more years, they were much more likely to be part of the problem than the solution. At the same time, new leaders do not need to pause to reenact a new structure. They can get rolling with a new approach quickly and build on what works.

TRY IT

1. Take any initiative in which you participate. Look carefully at the extent to which it has put results first. Then draft results that strike you as critical to achieve and motivating for participant groups.

2. Do a rough calculation of time spent by all groups participating in a collaboration of any form. If you are

typical, just use your time and average hourly cost and multiply by the number of other groups. Then compare the cost with the gain–both now and with result clarity you may need to add.

CHAPTER 19

Diversity, Equity, and Inclusion

Inequalities in achievement due to race, ethnicity, sex, and gender identity are unacceptable realities in every field. Graduation rates are lower, preventable deaths are higher, people of color are arrested and incarcerated at far higher rates than White people who commit the same crime. Females make less than males for the same job. On and on. Philanthropy and nonprofits repeat and underscore inequalities, but not much has changed to reduce or eliminate them.

My family has borne witness. Our kids include black and gay. We have watched them face obstacles and limits from a very young age and to carry a fearfulness we have never known.

Does DEI fit within a result framework, or is it a result in its own right? Both, I think. In part, this is a discussion of means and ends. It is an area where the goodness of the quest and its effectiveness in closing gaps and power disparities can diverge. If DEI increases greatly, but few more students of color read at grade level, is that enough? Reflecting diversity seems only the start. Harnessing differences to create solutions that cannot come from the like-minded is quite another. For me, the same question applies to other approaches and activities: So what? So we have diverse people at the table. Has this led to a reduction in the gap between ethnicities, sex, gender identities, and income levels? Are more people of color reading at grade level? Do more Black adults have a living wage job, a house, and food security?

Organizations often see hiring a Chief Equity Officer and placing them high on the org chart as an easy fix. Same question: what difference has that made? One that I frequently see first is that the chief equity person is the highest-ranking person of color in the organization. Also, the leader of DEI has an uneasy relationship with other departments. The premise is negative: "I am here to help you correct a fault by getting more diverse." How much more powerful is it to say that I am here to help us harness the power of diversity and equity to increase our achievement. I am here to help raise both morale and productivity. We all do better when we belong. I am here to help make that happen. Gap-closing on the ground, not on the organization chart.

Terms for Engagement

Many nonprofit words are warm and inviting. Programs are "seamless," individuals are "empowered," nonprofits are "mission driven," and we all aspire to be "collaborative." Definitions are even more important in DEI, where conferences and publications for foundations and nonprofits tend to put the words together. The shared definition is largely by value and sentiment. If we are to set and track targets for more of each term within DEI, some differentiation seems critical. Consider the term "diversity." Narrowly put, it means representation of race, ethnicity, sex, gender identities, and other key factors. My friend, Gayle Burnett, defines diversity more broadly as the range of human differences, including but not limited to race, ethnicity, sex, gender identity, sexual orientation, age, social class, physical ability or attributes, religious or ethical value systems, national origin, and political beliefs.

Equity can mean getting everyone to an equal level. Or it can mean starting with and preserving differences. All students at grade level on standardized tests reflect the former, while Native American language preservation reflects the latter. Inclusion can mean considering all viewpoints and honoring differences, or it can mean bringing everyone to the same inclusive viewpoint. Term meaning also intertwines with perspectives. Some programs, for example, ask if everyone is included. Others ask if people feel included.

I recently read "His Truth is Marching On," historian Jon Meacham's biography of Congressman John Lewis. I was reminded how this revered civil rights leader used words with great synergy of passion and clarity. Along with Martin Luther King Jr, he not only cherished language, but used it to set standards. Nonviolent means never violent. Love means always including those who despise you. Few words in DEI stand as unqualified as for these leaders. While the viewpoints of the people who use them can vary and change, the power of some words may well be that they are immutable and even absolute. In no area does that seem as critical as it does in DEI.

Getting clear on words is an essential starting point for defining and verifying achievement in this critical work.

Results for DEI

Just what constitutes more diversity, equity, and/or inclusion? What is present in a more diverse, equitable, and inclusive group that has less of these conditions? Nonprofits can answer. An example:

I led a study on great community health centers and what they did differently from groups deemed good or average by care and sustainability metrics. One health center deemed great focused on board meetings. The federally qualified centers were mandated to have half of their board mirror the composition of their patients. This center could see that the community representatives mostly sat on one side of the table, and the professionals on the other. They further observed that most time was spent by those on one side of the table asserting things to those on the other. This center created a great target: if a person who knows nothing of board composition sits in for 10 minutes of a board meeting, they cannot tell which members were the professionals and which were community representatives from the ways they speak and interact. The board members, together, figured out how to change that.

I like the broader question. What would you see within an organization and its programs when they are more inclusive? More equitable? More diverse?

One widely used result in DEI is reduction in gaps. Some look at gaps in available services. Others focus on a gap in access to resources. What if the services are ineffective? What if few see or use the opportunities available? The gap that matters is the gap in results.

With gaps, it is very important to get beneath averages. If we are looking at compensation differences, we could compare average salaries for different groups. The real story, however, lies in the extremes. The huge gap is between what those at the top and the bottom make. For a broader look at the severe limits of averaging, read Todd Rose's "The End of Average."[41]

All of the result tools in Part 1 apply to defining, tracking, and verifying achievements in DEI. If the premises contain cultural or other biases, put in different ones and modify the approach. Results first is a discipline, not the body of experience or even knowledge to which it is applied.

A significant challenge in setting DEI in a results frame is the justifiable focus on structural factors, which is discussed in Chapter 1. On the one hand, results are harder to state than ones for households and individuals, especially within a two- to three-year horizon. On the other hand, the intractable nature of these factors can lead to a shift away from the power of nonprofits to make systems change, even locally. Consider a nonprofit where 80% of its participants are people of color and only 3 of 15 board members reflect that demographic. The board sets a goal of changing that to 10 of 15. When this does not happen, the explanation I hear is that the problem is external. "We can't find qualified board members." How about revisiting what you mean by qualified? Is someone facing a problem qualified to speak to it? And how about an aggressive board development program that shifts from a focus on appropriate board behaviors to greatest possible help?

I even worry about the adages—such as time, talent, and treasures. A person with low income may have little time to give. They may have no treasure when it is defined as money and connections. And they may feel that talent is limited to traditional definitions. Why not break that mold? We tend not to solve problems where the fault is seen as lying beyond us.

Trust in Motion

"Change happens at the speed of trust." This is a fashionable line in philanthropy and nonprofit organizational writings. This sounds great, but does it mean people should wait a few years for a safe house or water line while we build trust?

I have worked with the self-help programs described in Chapter 7 for many years. These Native American, Black, Hispanic, and other minority groups had one thing in common. They were tired of their kids not doing well in school, living next to toxic waste, and lacking a primary doctor or clinic. Perhaps the most urgent need I saw was in colonias on the Texas-Mexican border, where one in three children would get Hepatitis by age 10 years due to the lack of running water. These residents did not want to take weeks or months to build relationships. They wanted their kids to stay healthy.

To overcome the vast gaps in privilege and well-being that often exist where DEI is lacking, I like motion. It is critical in areas ranging from weight control and health to overall wellness. People come alive with some form of action. We see that in people who need to actually handle the keyboard themselves to effectively learn a procedure an IT expert has just shown them.

Most change takes energy, which ties to motion in the term kinetic energy. Thesaurus.com defines kinetic energy as a, "form of energy that an object or particle has by reason of its motion." In DeI and all major change work, start with motion. Here is my belief: Trust happens at the speed of change.

TRY IT

1. Ask a few people to join you in making a list of what you see and hear when the organization has more diversity, equity, and/or inclusion.

2. Pick a gap that portrays great inequality in the geography and problem area you address. Define it with data points at the smallest possible scale for which any information can be found or generated. Ask if the gap or what to do to reduce it at the very local level is different in any way from that in the broader picture.

PART IV NOTES

36. The Hewlett Foundation report is by Prudence Brown and Leila Fiester and was published in March 2007. It was prepared under contract to the William and Flora Hewlett Foundation. The 12 pages of Summary at the beginning will give you the full picture. If you can't find it, email **info@results1st.com** and we will send it to you.

37. The CORAL report was commissioned by The James Irvine Foundation and was done by Gary Walker, past president of Public/Private Ventures. This 23 page report was published in May, 2007 in the Foundation's publication called Insight.

38. Shore describes 24 successful programs. While the approaches were important, most models were fueled by one or two people. This finding is highly useful. My friend and board member Peter Gerry is a venture capitalist. He told me that all business plans belong in the fiction section of the library. Their biggest value is to tell you about the entrepreneur who wrote it. When Dale Russakloff, in her book on the Newark schools covered in Chapter 10, describes fizzles, she speaks to major forces and policies. When she speaks to occasional bright spots, they seem to always start with a person. Shakel Nelson was a 5th grade math teacher and saw her students move from failing to passing tests. Her methods were personal and did not need to affect Newark wide. They just had to work in her classroom. People can bring success even within troubled large enterprises.

39. "Shared Minds" was ahead of its time when first published in 1990. Schrage, a Research Fellow at MIT's Sloan School of Management, created a distinct approach to innovation and how two or three individuals spark it. In later books such as "The Innovator's Hypothesis" (2014) he expands on the concept of using prototypes to guide collaboration. He writes, "The purpose of an experiment is not to solve the problem, but to generate insights."

40. Henry Ford once famously said that if he asked people what they needed, they would have said a faster horse. A huge limit of needs assessment is get-

ting beyond what is seen as possible. I actually like the different question—what do you want? I want to go faster. A horse is just one way of doing so.

41. This book is fascinating. Author Rose is eloquent on the two fatal flaws of designing goods and services for the average person. First, no one is actually average, especially when a variety of dimensions is considered. Second, "averaging" gets to a low bar. Few nonprofits have an aspiration for average gains for their participants. Averages also suggest sameness. Success for most of us is more distinctive.

PART V

Making Change

Activism is my rent for living on the planet.
— Alice Walker

I've found the cure for depression is action.
— Yvon Chouinard

I hope you have read something in this book you consider useful. If so, get a few actors and perform. A short one-act is the best place to start. Some of the steps can be tried in an hour at your next meeting or musing. What you need is the spark to act and the smarts to pick one or several teammates who are as eager to try something new as you are.

CHAPTER 20

The Road to Results First

I could conclude the book with sentiments. Good luck, results-seekers. Aspire to greatness. Trust in the process. Your journey begins. I would rather leave you with clarity on what you can do right now to put something from this book into motion.

From Sitting to Striding

Here are four simple steps to apply something you found of value in the book.

Define an Action

Pick something to do—anything you see as helping you and your organization put results first. You could start with one of the "Try Its" that conclude each chapter. Ones that I have seen work well:

- Write your own result description. Share it with a colleague or boss and ask them to do likewise. (Chapter 12)
- Shift the aiming point of a program or internal activity from an activity to a result. Just look at the top line statements. (Chapter 1)

- Try describing a program as having two parts: what you offer and what participants do with it. (Chapter 6)
- Take up the milestone of participant engagement and ask staff and a few participants to say what they see and hear in a person that signals engagement. (Chapter 3)
- Complete this sentence and try it the next time you are asked to introduce your group: "We are (name of group). Last year we (name your strongest achievement)." (Chapter 5)

Whatever you select, make sure it involves a behavior you control. Make sure you can define two to four steps you will take to try something and that you can take the first one within one week. Also, define the end point of this first try at something and what you will look for to see if it worked. The result could involve a group or team, but it could also just involve yourself.

Get a Partner or Small Team

Most of us do better if we have at least one person who helps us to take action. Pick a person whose role and/or personal attributes could be important for success—either in your small first effort or when it comes time to getting support to spread it. Roles your partner could play include:

- Helping you pick a first action that has a way forward if it works.
- Supporting you with both encouragement and as much of a push as you need.
- Verifying a change in your behavior. It is more important that others see it, not just yourself.

- Seeing possibilities and ways forward that you do not see.

Note that nothing is said about adding cautions or concerns or reminders that you need to be "realistic." That comes later, when a practice is ready to go wide and deep. At this point, you are just looking for one or two persons who know what you are going to do differently and are fully prepared to help.

Try Something

While some wait for a muse to strike for even small changes, others wisely see that they will generate more energy in themselves and others when moving. I have friends who successfully use this truth in many forms of work. Therapists talk with clients while walking. Staff consider a new strategic route while drawing on a map. Speakers go beyond traditional coffee breaks to integrating exercise and thinking.

The key is immediacy. If you read this book and decide you will do something once you get the time or space to do so next month, good luck. If you decide that you can do something Monday morning, luck is not necessary. The wonderful expression "Just do it" gains as much from the timetable as the imperative. Just do it means just do it now. It is fine to start by going downhill!

Keep Going

When you get to the end of a first tiny project, the temptation may be to either do a full stop or continue to do what you are now doing. Neither is as valuable as a short pause to see what is working and how to keep refining any changes that look promising. You can broaden and deepen in several ways. One is to involve more people to whom the new actions are clearly highly relevant. This gradual broadening can happen for as long as it takes to get a strong base for a new practice and, eventually, a tipping point that includes the mainstream and early adopters. Until that point is reached, it may be best to low-key your efforts, ensuring that you are at most trying incremental next steps, not transformation.

At some point in this broadening, you are ready to introduce change as a prototype project. This establishes assumptions to be tested, clear achievement metrics, and a way to see gains relative to those made in the traditional activities. At this point, you are in front of the curtain. You are ready to get actors and a script. Chapter 8 on innovating describes a process of scaling which may bring your first small acts to remarkable impact.

Who's on First?

In small behavior-change projects that show great promise, you will soon need other people to grow a practice. It really matters who you pick or encourage to be on a team. To best find these persons, I need to bring in a remarkable discovery about human behavior that was made some 70 years ago. It was developed by Everett Rogers and first applied to farmers asked to try new seed corn. He noted the patterns in responses by growers to innovations and called this the Diffusion of Innovation curve. Here it is:

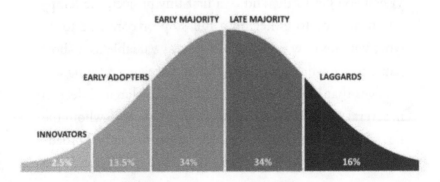

This curve suggests that when it comes to an uptake on anything new, people are divided into three groups that fall on a standard curve or distribution. The Early Adopters are those who will go first to try something new. They may well not have had the idea or have been first to lead the charge, but they will go first to help try something. At the opposite end are Laggards—those who resist change and often will never embrace it. "Show me, show me, show me, and I still won't try it." The mainstream is in the middle—early and late majority. People there won't go first or even second. But once those involved show that the risk is minimal, and people seem to like doing it, they will come aboard.

See if these distinctions work for you. Make a list of those persons with whom you work that fit the early adopter definition. Then make a list of laggards. I bet you will not find that difficult. You now have the group from which your first teammates for change will come. They are on first.

Join Results 1st in a Compact?

I have pointed out the difference between organizational agreements and personal commitments. I suggest a compact between you and my group, Results 1st.

You will:

1. Select something from this book you want to use and design a project to see if it works.
2. Let me know what it is and be receptive to my guidance when you are stuck or want additional help.
3. Get the project to the finish line.
4. Verify level of achievement.

Results 1st will:

1. Respond quickly to you every time you seek my help. If the demand exceeds my capability, I will hand-pick someone from Results 1st to engage with you.
2. Provide deeper information on tools and personal communication as needed.
3. Suggest other groups and projects from which I think you can learn and make introductions where useful.

4. Highlight your experience and success through my publications and the work of the company I created, Results 1st.

Just go to **www.results.1st.org** and the heading on *Put Results First* book readers. You will see an easy way to get us connected and rolling.

ACKNOWLEDGMENTS

My colleagues, clients, and supporters have become essential partners in designing and applying the tools and approaches in this book.

First to four mentors. The science-fiction writer, Issac Asimov, was a longtime friend who greatly influenced how I think of technology and progress. His three laws of robotics are highly useful in considering ethical implications of AI. Lewis Mumford, the social critic and observer, was equally blunt with me. Lewis helped me in the quest for reanimating the culture of small towns. My third mentor was Bert Swanson, a rare academic driven to apply what he wrote in "The Rulers and the Ruled" to the realities of life and culture in small settlements. My fourth guide was MIT's macro engineer, Frank Davidson. He made preposterously large projects first possible, then probable.

My colleague list includes virtually everyone I've worked with at The Rensselaerville Institute(TRI). Bill Phillips ran our innovation group and taught me that fresh thinking can happen in government. Arthur Webb, a senior commissioner for three New York governors, enriched my concepts for years—and still does. John LaRocca was our bellwether to stay not just positive but cheerful even with tough challenges. Jane Schautz led our community sparkplug work with relentless energy and joy. Irmgard Wogan deftly managed our office and the many divergent views contained therein.

Also at Rensselaerville comes the board, which was active in so many good ways. They constantly supported my quests for new directions, even when they suspected they would not work. Larry Bober persuaded the board to let us take on a large foundation loan to start the revitalization of Stump Creek. John Klingenstein was always there when we needed money or moral support. Oscar Straus, Bill Engel, Diane Schaffer, and Skip Rankin provided encouragement and boundaries. I loved the first and needed the second.

Clients—the list is far too long to include everyone. Here are a few that went on to play key roles at TRI. Ross Swimmer, former Principal Chief of the Cherokee Nation, Tom Ross, former CEO of the Z Smith Reynolds Foundation, and MK Larson head of the MR and Eveyln Hudson Foundation became Institute Trustees who brought clear views of philanthropy. Les Loomis, an accomplished public school superintendent, kept me engaged with school leaders up against strong traditions. Roxie Jerde has been a partner in both the Greater Kansas City and Sarasota Community Foundation in nudging donors to look at the actual difference their money made. Charles Hamilton, head for years of the Clark Foundation in New York City offered his considerable insight on foundations. I was once told to keep your clients and your friends distinct. I am so glad I ignored that advice.

Among my best business decisions was to choose Robyn Faucy as my bet for not just keeping but refining and spreading my small legacy in the world of outcomes. I created Results 1st, and she leads it. I smile when I hear her talk firmly to prospects who do not know what they want to achieve. Robyn is building an impressive team of consultants and following in my path of getting many of my best ideas and applications from those we seek to help invest in results and spend money to achieve them. Her results speak loudly at Results1st.org.

My family is not just the center of my life, but integral in my thinking and writing about results. Pam, my wife, pushes me to make more sense and edits my biweekly blog entries. Once she became a lawyer, I had to start defining my terms. And her love has reminded me that some things are an outcome just by being present. My daughter Gillian and I worked closely together to form School Turnaround, based on her remarkable achievements as a very young principal in New York City schools. For years it has been the signature program of TRI and a singular force for clarity for me. She also helped greatly in responding to a draft of this book.

The personal side brought laughter and insight over many years. "What's the outcome for today, pal?" asked my son, Ben. "What's leadership in an orchestra or music ensemble?" asked my son, Jeremy. Jessica brought result clarity in her field of educational psychology and reminded me that equal treatment of people with specific needs does not mean treating them all the same. Denise joined our diverse family at age 13 years and brought fresh eyes and a wealth of opportunity to revisit old stories while she was with us making new ones.

Finally, appreciation to James Hytner, my editor, and Troy Book Makers who provided the book design. Both know their trade very well.

Hal Williams
January 2024

——— **ADVANCE PRINTING, JANUARY, 2024.** ———

This advance edition of Put Results First seeks to generate reader reflections on value and to spot passages that are not clear. Please let me know on either front at **HAL@RESULTS1ST.ORG**